# Roman Capitalism
# and
# Revelation

**Biblical Hermeneutics Rediscovered**

The Series as the name suggests will focus on Biblical Hermeneutics, i.e., literary works concerned with methods of interpreting the Old and New Testaments of Bible via different stream of topics like Literature & Poetry, Indigenous Philosophizing, Ethical response towards Ecology, Health & Healing, Science & Technology, Feminist Theology, Sociological approach towards Human Rights, Law & Politics, Arts, History of Ideas, Ancient Civilizations, Cultural Contiguity, Religious Cosmologies & Mysticism, Appraisal of various Theologians, World Peace & Harmony, Global Capitalism, Network Marketing, Cybertheology, Population & Demographics, Epigraphic Studies, Contextualized Education, and many others. We welcome a Mss. on any topic/s mentioned, whether they are original works, scholarly monographs, collections of conference papers, revised dissertations, or translations of historical documents. Through the Series we, the Publishers, are striving to put forward published works that may help Institutions, Academic Bodies, Researchers, Scholars and the World at large in furthering their respective knowledge and understanding on the concerned subject. We welcome your comments on our efforts and further suggestions on how we can enshrine new ray of analysing & explaining the written Texts through our upcoming books.

*Biblical Hermeneutics Rediscovered - 37*

# Roman Capitalism and Revelation

PC Nghaklianmawia

Christian World Imprints

First Published in 2020 by

**Christian World Imprints**
*Christian Publishing & Books from India*
C-3, Wazirpur Industrial Area
**Delhi-110052**
cwidelhi2017@gmail.com
www.ChristianWorldImprints.com
Phone: +91 11 41526079

ISBN: 978-93-5148-478-3 (HB)
ISBN: 978-93-5148-479-0 (PB)



Printed in India.

Appendix-2

# A Map of the Roman Trade in the First Century

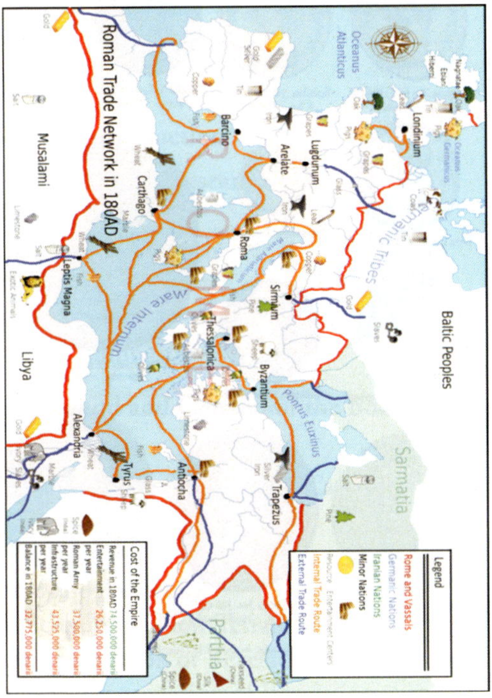


## *Reference*

*https://commons.wikimedia.org/wiki/File:Europe_180ad_roman_trade_map.png.*

That the book in its original form is the thesis submitted to the *Senate of Serampore College*, towards the M.Th degree and is published with written permission. The candidate is responsible for the title, contents and opinions expressed in it.The Original title of the thesis is "De-empowerment of Economic Capitalism in the fall of Babylon as reflected in Revelation 18"

# Foreword

Rev. PC Nghaklianmawia's book "***Roman Capitalism and Revelation*** is an upgraded version of his MTh Thesis guided by me in 2017-2019 at the United Theological College, Bangalore. He has been a very systematic researcher with a critical and reflective thinking framework which enables him to be a pioneer in the field of New Testament studies. I am delighted to state that he has developed skills in terms of becoming an excellent researcher in the field of New Testament. As we encounter new challenges and issues, it is important to have new sensible studies to reveal the basics of the Scripture and its meaning.

This book is a systematic and open-minded study of the book of Revelation 18 from a post-colonial and political viewpoint. The author has brilliantly surveyed the origin and development of the book of Revelation and its place in the New Testament canon. Further, he explained the history of interpretation of the book of Revelation which could touch almost all areas of interpretation. In our context, the message of apocalyptic literature seems to be significant in the message can change the status quo as well as the oppressive structure of the imperial powers.

Therefore, it is important to explore and explain the theology of the book of Revelation for understanding the hegemonic dimensions of the imperial power and structures especially in terms of economic exploitation. I am sure this book will offer significant insights for developing a relevant hermeneutical principle for studying the New Testament books. I sincerely hope and pray that

Rev. PC Nghaklianmawia will regularly contribute to the Indian Christian Biblical scholarship. With a real sense of passion I present this book.

**Rev. Dr. Prof. C. I. David Joy**
Principal, KUTS
Board Member SBLICI (2020 - till date)
Editorial Board IVBSSBL (2017 - till date)

# Acknowledgements

This book is an updated version of the MTh thesis which was submitted to Senate of Serampore College (University) in 2019 under the original title, "De-empowerment of Economic Capitalism in the fall of Babylon as Reflected in Revelation 18". This work has been blessed by various supports and well-wishes. First and foremost, I thank almighty God for enabling me and guiding me throughout my theological journey.

I am deeply grateful and indebted to my Professor, Rev. Dr. C.I. David Joy, a well-known Indian Biblical scholar who specialized in the post-colonial approach of the Bible. His excellent guidance and help gave me an inspiration of theological zeal especially in the field of New Testament studies. The study would not have been completed without his cooperation and constant encouragement. Indeed, I am honored to say that he is my mentor and inspiration who guides and encouraged me in various capacities. His sincerity and commitments, cooperation, and stimulating suggestions define his excellence as a teacher which I greatly admire. I acknowledge my heartfelt gratitude for his meaningful foreword.

I also express my sincere gratitude to the Principal of United Theological College, as well as to all the Professors and staffs for their cooperation and support throughout this research. I specially thanked my Professors in New Testament department for their valuable teachings and the staffs of the college library for enabling me to access the library with patience. They are important figures that made our life in the campus comfortable and worthwhile. I would also like to express my sincere thanks to the Senate of Serampore College (University) for giving me permission to publish my research. Moreover, my sincere thanks to Dr. J.C. Zomuanthanga, Mizoram University for helping me in editing and writing valuable comments on this research.

I am deeply indebted to my parents and family for their prayers, encouragement and support. I dedicated this small work to my beloved father Bawihthanga, who left for his heavenly abode on November 25, 2017 during the course of my research work. His untimely demise instills a sense of grief and bewilderment. He had eagerly and impatiently waited for the completion of my M.Th. studies. However, God loves him more than us and had brought him to his permanent address.

Besides, I am also immensely delighted to mention the love and sacrifices of my beloved wife, Janet Lalnunhlui, and my two precious sons, PC Vanlaldika and Lalrinawma Pachuau who deserved my sincere gratitude and affection. They spared me enough time enabling me to do my hectic research work without any hindrance. Indeed, they share my burden, passion, pressure and the blessing involved in this work. They are the important cornerstones in the success of this research.

My sincere gratitude goes to Mizoram Presbyterian Church Synod for sponsoring me financially and allowing me to pursue my theological studies. I also sincerely appreciate Christian World Imprints for their willingness to take up the task of publishing the book for the benefits of Christian literature.

Above all, my sincere gratitude to the Almighty God who blessed me through this work and it is my prayers that many will profit from this work too.

**PC Nghaklianmawia**

# List of Abbreviation

| | | |
|---|---|---|
| ABD | - | The Anchor Bible Dictionary |
| AUSS | - | Andrews University Seminary Studies |
| APSR | - | American Political Science Review |
| BCE | - | Before Common Era |
| BBC | - | Broadman Bible Commentary |
| BNT | - | Bible Works New Testament |
| CE | - | Common Era |
| CBQ | - | Catholic Bible Quarterly |
| CTQ | - | Concordia Theological Quarterly |
| Chr | - | Chronicles |
| DBI | - | Dictionary of Biblical Interpretation |
| DSS | - | Dead Sea Scroll |
| DOB | - | Dictionary of the Bible |
| DLNTD | - | Dictionary of Later New Testament and Its Development |
| DNTB | - | Dictionary of New Testament Background |
| Deut | - | Deuteronomy |
| EDNT | - | Exegetical Dictionary of the New Testament |
| Ezek | - | Ezekiel |
| Exod | - | Exodus |
| Fasc | - | Facsimile |
| HBT | - | Horizons in Biblical Theology |
| HTR | - | Harvard Theological Review |
| HBD | - | Harpers' Bible Dictionary |
| ISBE | - | International Standard Bible Encyclopaedia |

| | | |
|---|---|---|
| ICC | - | International Critical Commentary |
| IVPDNT | - | IVP Dictionary of the New Testament |
| JRS | - | Journal of Roman Studies |
| JSNT | - | Journal for the Study of New Testament |
| JBS | - | Journal of Biblical Studies |
| JEI | - | Journal of Economic Issue |
| JBL | - | Journal of Biblical Literature |
| JRE | - | Journal of Religious Ethics |
| Jer | - | Jeremiah |
| Lev | - | Leviticus |
| LXX | - | Septuagint |
| Matt | - | Matthew |
| MDB | - | Mercer Dictionary of the Bible |
| NICNT | - | New International Commentary on New Testament |
| NIGTC | - | The New International Greek Testament Commentary |
| NIDB | - | New Interpreters' Dictionary of the Bible' |
| NRSV | - | New Revised Standard Version |
| NT | - | New Testament |
| NIV | - | New International Version |
| OT | - | Old Testament |
| Prov | - | Proverb |
| Ps | - | Psalm |
| RSV | - | Revised Standard Version |
| Rev | - | Revelation |
| TNTC | - | Tyndale New Testament Commentary |
| TEV | - | Today's English Version |
| UNESCO | - | The United Nations Educational, Scientific and Cultural Organization |
| v | - | Verse |
| vv | - | Verses |
| WBC | - | Word Biblical Commentary |

Chapter 1

# General Introduction

## 1.1. Background of the Research

This research is an attempt to give a critique of the unjust socio-economic structure of the Roman Empire found in Revelation 18. The Roman Empire was socially and economically hierarchical, and the spirits of commercialism cause cities to become swollen along with people who increase crime, violence, corruption, and poverty. Therefore, this research intends to critically examine the unjust socio-economic-political situation of the Roman Empire and its implication for our contemporary.

## 1.2. An Elaboration

The Book of Revelation is written in the form of the apocalyptic genre. It is concerned with both religious purity and with issues of social justice and economic exploitation.[1] Apocalyptic writing employs dramatic symbolism to describe events, persons and corporate entities (e.g. cities, nations etc.). These symbols tend to be highly visual in nature and are designed to evoke strong emotions.

1 James Benedict, "The Great Whore Cast Down Revelation 17-18 and the Imagery of Roman Conquest." *Brethren Life and Thought*, 61 No. 1 (Spring 2016), 39-48.

In Revelation 18, the portrayal of 'the fall of Babylon' is a metaphor of the Roman Empire; Revelation focuses its attack not Babylon's architecture or physical layout, but on its trade and alliances. The luxurious life and love of money brings a forged corruption in the society; misuse of power and authority are found in the Roman Empire. Rome was a World Trade Centre, an economic engine of the world, controlling vast territories and peoples and amazing great wealth through its shipping and trade.[2] Under the empire, we see the economic changes both the inequality and reciprocity that were embedded in the Roman Empire. Economic exchanges between center and periphery, metropolis and the margins, imperial and colonial as doomed. These sorts of connections are also evident, today, by way of globalization - a process that reach across diverse cultural, ethnic, and racial identities, while also creating 'inside/ outside' boundaries within which our identities are contested, challenged, and often jeopardized at each turn by strife and scarcity, dealing death as often as life.[3]

The Roman power was depended on the strength of military and economic. Great power, wealth, and status resided in the hands of very small ruling elite. As the parables of Jesus indicate (cf. Mark 12:1-12; Matt. 20:1-16), land provided the basis of wealth. The empire had a proprietary economy, with the emperor asserting control over land (and Sea) by claiming a share of all produce (such as crops and livestock) through taxes and tributes. It was thus also a tributary economy, in that these taxes and tributes were paid in goods rather than cash. Historians debate the precise levels of taxation, but for small farmers trying to sustain extended families and pay multiple levels of taxes and rents to imperial, regional, and local powers, the impact could be severe. Although, elites conspicuously consumed and displayed wealth, most folks lived much less opulent lives. Some experience a level of comfort and security, but most, especially those

---

2 Barbara R. Rossing, *The Choice Between Two Cities-Whore, Bride, and Empire in the Apocalypse* Harvard Theological Studies (USA: Trinity Press International, 1999), 117.

3 Rohun Park, "Revelation for Sale: An Intercultural Reading of Revelation 18 from an East Asian Perspective" *The Bible and Critical Theory*, Volume-4, (No. 2, 2008), 251.

with few or no skills and only their labour to sell, lived precariously around and below subsistence levels, as described in Matthew 25:31-46.[4] Babylon (Roman Empire) is also called as economic exploiter in Revelation 18 because the character of Babylon as depicted as an attachment to wealth in Rev. 18. The collapse of economic power brings the destruction of the empire. The reasons might be the luxurious and corrupted life, and, this luxurious is parallel to the accusation of self-glorification. This verb and the equally rare noun "luxury" carry connotations both of luxurious consumption and also of sexual license and arrogance.[5] Many of the items listed in the destruction of the city are specifically mentioned as prime examples of luxury and extravagance by the Roman elites.

A burning city is symbolical of the fall of the whole powerful commercial system because of the sins committed. C. I. David Joy further mentions that Rome represents "the culmination of all evil structures and forces including a luxurious lifestyle. The evil dimensions of Rome (Babylon) can be found in any imperial dominant rules in the world. The metaphor of Babylon somehow refers to the processor state of idolatry, misuse of power, sexual abuse and disorder, corruption and dehumanising activities of the Roman Empire."[6] All these sins were inter-related each other, and the concern people like kings, merchant, sailors are all collaborated with Rome. The corrupted and inhuman life of the ruling small elite affects the poor and the marginalised. The prosperity of Rome leads to a luxurious life, misuse of power, money worship, ignoring poor and the victim often always the poor and marginalized. Therefore, the entire chapter of Rev. 18 makes clear that Babylon is judged principally as a centre of unjust wealth and predatory trade; Rome has benefited the merchants of the earth at the expense of many suffering people.[7] The above mention clearly portrays that the unjust

4 Warren Carter, "Economic Justice and the Roman Empire" n.p. [Cited 11 July 2017]. Online: http://www.bibleodyssey.org/en/passages/related-articles/economic-justice-and-the-roma n-empire.

5 Rossing, *The Choice Between Two Cities,* 126.

6 C. I. David Joy, *Revelation-A Post-colonial View Point* (Delhi: ISPCK, 2001), 77-78.

7 Rossing, *The Choice Between Two Cities*, 115.

socio-economic condition of the Roman Society. Therefore, the main attempt of this research is to address and critique the unjust economic structure of the Roman Empire in light of a critique of the eyes of economic capitalism.

## 1.3. Purpose of the Research

Revelation is a particularly apt text for ideological criticism, this ideological critique inquires about the possibilities of a just society and what that society would be like.[8] Economic Capitalism is one of the sovereign authorities to control, dominated and oppressed other social structure since the early centuries. Wealth is a power too; those who hold it have more power than generals with armies in ancient history. So, John could see the corrupting power of wealth; men worshipped material wealth as they bowed to Roma.[9] The divine Roman hierarchy can be seen as legitimating the system that transferred wealth from the many poor to the elite few.[10] The economic capitalism and its allies created a serious problem within the society as found in the Roman Empire and can become a threat to the future which is needed to address.

## 1.4. Methodology

Since the research attempt to critique the Roman Empire and its economic structure by giving socio-theological implications of Indian context, the Socio-Rhetorical method from Postcolonial lens is most appropriate and employed for doing this research. Socio-rhetorical criticism is an approach to literature that focuses on values, convictions, and beliefs both in the texts we read and in the world in which we lived, it invites detailed attention to the text itself.[11]

8 Robert M. Royalty, Jr. "Don't Touch this Book! Revelation 22:18-19 and the Rhetoric of Reading (in) the Apocalypse of John" *Biblical Interpretation-A Journal of Contemporary Approaches* Volume XII 3 (2004), 285.

9 Clifton J. Allen, ed., *Revelation. The Broadman Bible Commentary Volume 12* (Nashville: Broadman Press, 1972), 335.

10 Wes Howard Brook and Anthony Gwyther, *Unveiling Empire-Reading Revelation Then and Now* (4th Printing; New York: Orbis Books, 2002), 97.

11 Vernon K. Robbins, *Exploring the Texture of Texts-A guide to Socio-rhetorical Interpretation* (Pennsylvania: Trinity Press International, 1996), 1.

It also a multi-dimensional approach to texts guided by a multi-dimensional hermeneutic.[12] Further, it is an approach that evaluates and reorients its strategies and it engages in multi-faceted dialogue with the texts and other phenomena that comes within its purview, which means that it invites methods and methodological results into the environment of its activities, but those methods and results were always under scrutiny.[13] Thus, this research had done under the method of socio-rhetorical analysis with the help of a postcolonial lens; rhetorical reading brings the connection between the text and the social setting of the background. This method focuses on the analysis of social and economic dynamics which clearly depicts the unjust economic issues inside the text.[14] The rhetorical reading of the text gives us a deeper knowledge of issues behind the text and a profound understanding of the socio-political-economic milieu of the context of Roman Imperialism. And, it became the most appropriate method to address the unjust economic issues of the Roman economy in Rev. 18.

## 1.5. Previous Research

A number of researches had been done in relation to the book of Revelation and its related topics. Gummalolla Soleman done his DTh *Thesis* under the title of "*Postcolonial Interpretation of Apocalyptic Symbolism as a mode of Resistance in Revelation*" in 2016.[15] The genre of apocalyptic literature was given emphasis and also employs a postcolonial reading of the text in this research. B. S. Shasikala did *The Portrayal of 'Rome' in the Book of Revelation: A Search for*

---

12 Vernon K. Robbins, '*Socio Rhetorical Hermeneutics and Commentary*' EPI TO AYTO. Essays in honour of Petr Pokorny on his 65th birthday, Edited by J. Mrazek, S Brodsky, and R. Dvorakova. (Praha-Trebenice: Mlyn Publishers, 1998), 284-297.

13 Vernon K. Robbins, "Socio-Rhetorical Interpretation" in *The Blackwell Companion to the New Testament* Edited by David Aune (London: Wiley Blackwell, 2010), 192.

14 Robbins, "Socio-Rhetorical Interpretation," 192.

15 Soleman, Gummalolla, *Postcolonial Interpretation of Apocalyptic Symbolism as a mode of Resistance in Revelation* (DTh Thesis, Senate of Serampore College, 2016).

*a Liberative Paradigm for the Subaltern Communities*, MTh Thesis, Senate of Serampore College, 2013. She gives a detail explanation of portrayal of 'Rome' in Revelation by mentioning the destruction of Babylon (Rome) with a conclusion of globalisation impacts. Joseph Samuel wrote in his MTh Thesis entitled '*Wealth and Possession' in the Gospel According to Luke: An early Christian Alternative to Roman Imperial Economy*, Senate of Serampore College, 2010. He focuses on the Roman imperial economic condition by emphasizing the economic issues from the Gospel of Luke. He deals on the position of the poor and its related to the economic gap with the rich. As per the finding of a researcher, no particular research from the selected text and theme related to this has been done so far.

## 1.6. Scope and Limitation

This research mainly focused on the analysis of the unjust political-economic structure of the Roman Empire as found in Revelation; a brief survey of the book of Revelation and its related genre of apocalyptic literature also employed along with a critique of Economic Capitalism in Roman Imperial system and its related issues. The research may be limited with a deeper study of an apocalyptic genre that helps us to understand the core idea of the book and the present juncture is lacking in the research due to limited space, also the biblical hermeneutics of socio-rhetorical reading may need to improve.

Chapter 2

# Background and Context of the Book of Revelation

## 2.1. Introduction

This chapter introduces the book of Revelation and its background along with portraying the authorship debate and controversial discussion of dating which gives us a new insight of the book; historical interpretation and canonicity which tells us the unique identity of the book and the theology of Revelation which signifies the contemporary situation of the book. Besides, the apocalyptic genre of the book of Revelation was also discussed in this chapter.

The title 'Revelation' was first found in the oldest textual witness (Codex Sinaiticus) as it gives 'Revelation of John" as its title. This title is also found in Codex Alexandrinus (5th Century) the best witness, along with Codex Ephraemi (also 5th Century), to the text of this work. Other *mss* contain the titles, "Revelation of John, the one who speaks about God;" "Revelation of Saint John, the one who speaks about God;" "Revelation of John, the one who speaks about God, [the] evangelist;" and "The Revelation of the Apostle John, the Evangelist. The work may have already been known by the title "Revelation of John" in the 2nd Century. The Muratorian Canon (ca. 200 C.E.) states, "We receive also the apocalyptic works, only [those] of John and Peter." In the 2nd Century, however, the work may simply have been known as "Revelation." It is likely that the work at first had no separate title and that the opening words aroused the appropriate expectations in the audience by designating the nature of its contents: "A revelation of Jesus Christ." The meaning is "a revelation given by Jesus Christ," as the following words show ("that God gave to him [Jesus Christ] to show to his servants"). This is the first time that the Greek word "revelation" was used to describe a written work or even an explicitly visionary experience. When the book was copied unto scrolls, a brief title was added at the end of the work, probably "Revelation of John." When the work began to copy on book-like codices with pages, this title was placed at the beginning. In the course of transmission, the older, brief title was expanded in various ways.[16]

## 2.2. Date, Authorship, Purpose and Canonicity

### *Date*

The earliest external evidence accepted by most scholars is that of Irenaeus (ca. 180 C.E.). He says that John wrote his book near the end of Domitian's reign (81-96 C.E.).[17] C. I. David Joy also supports by saying the possible date could be during the reign of the Roman Emperor, Domitian (Circa 81-96 CE).[18] The principal reason for dating the book during this reign to the fact, that it contains a number of indications that become widespread in Domitian's day. These references are to the universal worship demanded by the beast, which is held to represent the Roman emperor (13:4, 12, 15; 14:9, 11; 15:2; 16:20; 20:4).[19] This point seems reasonably clear. But at the same time, some scholar (like Catherine and Justol L. Gonzalez) suggests that it should be either earlier as early as the reign of Nero

16 Adela Yarbro Collins, "Revelation, Book of," *ABD*: 694-695).

17 John Sweet, *Revelation* (London: SCM Press, 1990), 21.

18 Joy, *Revelation-A Post-colonial Viewpoint,* x.

19 C. L. Morris, *The Revelation of St. John: An Introduction and Commentary* (London: Tyndale Press, 1969), 35.

in 64 C.E. or slightly later.[20] German scholar Jurgen Roloff puts it between 90-95 C.E.[21] Some ancient tradition also says that it was written under Trajan (98-117 C.E.), or under Nero (54-68 C.E.).[22] Scholars like Lightfoot, Westcott, and Hort support the dating under Nero because they argued that it reflects the persecution under Nero rather than Domitian. They also point to 11:1, where the temple and Jerusalem appear still to be standing.[23] Despite the arguments of both Nero's and Domitian's reign of authorship date, most scholars agreed that the later date (Domitian's reign) is to be preferred.

## *Authorship*

Scholars are debating the authorship of the book. The traditional belief of the author is an apostle John as it has been revealed to the first chapter of the book: "The revelation of Jesus Christ, which God gave him to show his servants what must soon take place; he made it known by sending his angel to his servant John" (1:1 NRSV). The various assumptions had been made of authorship: Dionysius of Alexandria said that John Mark was possibly the author. Eusebius describes him as the Elder. Irenaeus designated John the disciple of the Lord as its author,[24] followed by early church fathers like Justin Martyr, Irenaeus, Clement of Alexandria, Tertullian and the Muratorian fragment also speaks twice of the author as John.[25] The Reformers Luther, Zwingli, and Erasmus also rejected it as non-apostolic.[26] It was Irenaeus (c. 180 C.E.), the one who proposed first of Apostle Authorship, he shared his ideas with Melito of Sardis and Justin Martyr and most later writers. He also believed that this same John also wrote the Fourth Gospel and the Johannine Epistles and

20 Catherine Gunsalus Gonzâlez and Justol L. Gonzâlez, *Revelation* (Louisville: John Knox Press, 1997), 8.

21 Jurgen Roloff, *Revelation-A Continental Commentary* Translated by John E. Alsup (Minneapolis: Fortress Press, 1993), 10.

22 Sweet, *Revelation,* 21.

23 Ladd, "Revelation, Book of" *ISBE*: 172.

24 T. S. Kepler, "Revelation, Book of" *DOB:* 849-50.

25 Morris, *The Revelation of St. John,* 26.

26 Henry Clarence Thiessen, *Introduction to the New Testament* (Fourth Edition; Grand Rapids: Eerdmans, 1948), 316.

that he was released from Patmos and lived on into Trajan's reign (98-117 C.E.); this view was widely held in the early church.[27] While Eusebius explains there are two Johns of John the disciples and John the elder, Eusebius regarded the first (John the disciples) as the author of the Gospel and the second (John the elder) as the author of Revelation.[28]

Scholars are careful to give a specific identity of the author; rather they proposed the identity and characteristics of the author from the study of the book of Revelation as follows:

1) he was possibly a Jew well versed in Scripture;
2) he had perhaps learned Greek rather late in life, as is evidenced by his often-awkward Greek style;
3) he was a church leader, well known to the seven churches of the province of Asia;
4) he was a deeply religious man, with great faith in the ultimate victory of the Christian religion over the demonic forces of the world;
5) he was not an eye witness of Jesus, for he never refers to the personal reminiscences of Jesus' life, and never indicates himself as an apostle or disciple; he refers to himself as a servant and a brother;
6) he was a literary genius, his skilled artistry giving us one of the most important and beautiful of the apocalypses.[29]

Scholars are also debating authorship, Ramsay supported the Johannine authorship as he assumed that John had an intimate knowledge of the Asian cities, to which the seven letters were addressed, in their past history and present circumstances. Ramsay's work had been confirmed and amplified by the first-hand investigations of

27 Sweet, *Revelation,* 36.

28 "And if anyone chanced to come who had actually been a follower of the elders, I would inquire as to the discourse of the elders, what Andrew or what Peter said, or what Philip, or what Thomas or James, or what John or Matthew or any other of the Lords' disciples [said]; and the things which Aristion and John the elder, disciples of the Lord, say. (As quoted by David Aune, *Revelation-WBC* Volume 52 (Texas: Word Books Publishers, 1997), liii).

29 T.S. Kepler, "Revelation, Book of" *Dictionary of the Bible*, Edited by James Hastings. Second Edition; Edinburgh: T&T Clark, 1963), 850.

C. J. Hemer.[30] Meanwhile, M. Kiddle states that the authorship of the Revelation may prove to be the one mystery of the book which will never be revealed in this world. W. G. Kummel also concluded that nothing is known about the author of the Apocalypse other than that he was a Jewish Christian prophet by the name of John.[31] The question of common authorship of Gospel and Revelation is uncertain. Many scholars in the nineteenth century, and most in the twentieth rejected traditional authorship. F. Hitzig (1843) argued for John Mark as the author, and Lohmeyer (1926) suggested John the Elder. According to J. Ford (1975), most of the book is a product of the John the Baptist circle, to which a Christian redactor has made additions; however, some scholars, including Allo and I. Beckwith (1919), have favoured the traditional view. Although, rejecting apostolic authorship, Lohmeyer argued that the author also wrote John's Gospel and the Johannine Letters.[32] Despite the controversial arguments made by scholars, most scholars comfort to put it as the author of John the Apostle.

## *Purpose and Audience*

The primary purpose of the book is to deliver the Lord's message to the early Christian community. The first century Christians were under the persecution of Roman Imperialism. It is learned that, according to Tacitus, some Christians in Rome were persecuted by Nero, and that Clement of Rome refers to oppressions, perhaps also those during Nero's time. After Nero died, he was succeeded by Galba (68 C.E.), Otho and Vitellius, and later Domitian became emperor of Rome, during his time, he commanded his family to address him as "our Lord and God" and publicized emperor worship. He was the first emperor who encourages the cult worship in the East. Therefore, they may have been some capricious persecution of Christians in Asia Minor near the end of his reign, although there

30 Sweet, *Revelation,* 38-39.

31 G. R. Beasley-Murray, "Revelation, Book of" *IVPDNT*: 924-936.

32 A. W. Wainwright, "Revelation, Book of" *DBI:* 393.

is no direct evidence for it.[33] Under those critical and hardships circumstances, God's revelation through His message is true medicine for the persecuted and oppressed community. H. B. Swete also remarks, it is a genuine outcome of the time, written with a view to a special need of a particular group of Christian societies; it portrays the life of those societies, and ministers to their spiritual necessities.[34] Bauckham also opines that the book is written for the consolation and encouragement of Christians suffering persecution, in order to assure them that their oppressors will be judged and they will be vindicated in the end.[35] In expand to this, Steve Moyise also analyse the book as an interpretation plays a crucial role for pursuing the author's intension, he asserts that scholars cannot agree whether John wrote to comfort the persecuted or challenge the complacent. Genre is said to be vital for interpretation, but scholars' debate whether Revelation is best seen as an apocalypse, a prophecy or a circular letter.[36] He further concludes that Revelation shares all three features. Despite the scholars' comments, traditional understanding avails that the intension of Revelation focuses on the addressing of the crucial context of the day.

In those days, each of the Churches of Asia had difficulties peculiar to itself, and these problems are treated first and this message (apocalypse) was delivered to them. Furthermore, the addressees of the author are the congregations with which the author had contact, congregations in the western edge of the province of Asia. All of these congregations are on the main road or on roads out of Ephesus that connects this region.[37] In addition, the socio-economic life of the people was very much imbalanced by comparing the life of ruling

---

33 Edwin D. Freed, *The New Testament: A Critical Introduction.* Second Edition; USA: Wadsworth Publishing Company, 1991, 369-70.

34 Henry Barclay Swete, *The Apocalypse of St. John: The Greek Text with Introduction Notes and Indices* (New York: Macmillan Company, 1906), xci.

35 Richard Bauckham, *The Theology of the Book of Revelation* (Reprinted; New York: Cambridge University Press, 1993), 15.

36 Steve Moyise, "Authorial Intension and the Book of Revelation" Andrews University Seminary Studies, *Spring*, Vol. 39. No. 1, (2001), 35-40.

37 Ben Witherington III, *Revelation- The New Cambridge Bible Commentary* (UK: Cambridge University Press, 2003), 7.

elites and the common people like peasants etc. Richard Horsley rightly comments the image of economic imbalance as the exchange of goods and services in patron-client relations stands diametrically opposed to the horizontal associations and reciprocity embodied in kinship and villages.[38] The economic system was facilitated for the political elite by commercial elite along with the lower class people were neglected and oppressed. Thus, the intention of the author through his writing was to help these churches to get through a dark period of oppression and suppression under the Roman imperialism. In similar to this view, A. Boesak rightly wrote: "Because of their political perception and challenge in such dangerous times, these books could not be written in the 'normal' way. Any person who has ever lived under political oppression, where every move is watched and every word carefully weighed and where every other person could be an informer knows this. Therefore, these books were written in a way that only the initiated could really understand and draw encouragement from. These books were, in the real sense of the word, underground protest literature."[39]

The great tragedy in the church today is that Revelation is narrowly and incorrectly interpreted with an obsessive focus on the future end times only. To address this issue, G. K. Beale also opines that the goal of Revelation is to bring encouragement to believers of all ages that God is working out His purposes even in the midst of tragedy, suffering and apparent Satanic domination.[40] He also concluded that the final reward is certain of those who put their trust in God despite the trials and temptations to march to the world's drumbeat.

## *Canonicity in the New Testament*

Because of its unique literary genre, apocalyptic theological discourse and style Revelation becomes a complex issue in the NT books, many

38 Richard Horsley, *Paul and Empire: Religion and Power in Roman Imperial Society* (Harrisburg: Trinity Press International, 1997), 90.

39 A. Boesak, *Comfort and Protest: The Apocalypse from a South African Perspective* (Philadelphia: Westminster, 1986), 19.

40 G. K. Beale, *Revelation-A shorter Commentary* (Grand Rapids: Eerdsman Publishing Company, 2015), 1.

of early church fathers hesitated to include as NT canon. But, still, the early church fathers knew and used Revelation in their works. According to Andreas, the archbishop of Caesarea in Cappadocia, Papias knew and commented on the book of Revelation. Papias flourished in the first half of the 2nd century.[41] Eusebius did not argue in favour of the book's status as a genuine part of the NT. Cyril of Jerusalem (4th Century) omitted from his list of books in the NT. Further, the Council of Laodicea in Phrygia, held in the mid-4th century also omitted Revelation from its list of the books of NT.[42]

At the beginning of the fourth century, opinion was divided about the book's canonical status and hesitation continued in the East. Cyril of Jerusalem did not include it in his canon. The Syrian church was reluctant to accept it; it was not included in the Peshitta, although it appeared in some later Syriac NTs.[43] Despite various disputes of canonicity, when Athanasius included Revelation in his list of NT books and the list was accepted as canon in 367 C.E. Thus, by the end of the fourth century, the book of Revelation was included in all the New Testament canons officially sanctioned by the church councils (Council of Hippo 393 and Council of Carthage 397).[44] Therefore, it is indeed no doubt that Revelation was later included in the canon among other books certainly because of its unique theology, genre and literary style, it creates a lot of controversial debatable issues for the accepting the book as NT canon.

## 2.3. Nature of the Book of Revelation

It is asserted and focused that Revelation is written for comforting of the oppressed. The book was presented in the form of the apocalyptic genre which is a common transmission during the early Christian centuries especially under the circumstances of oppression and exploitation. Costa Rican author Pablo Richard claims that Revelation arises in a time of persecution-and particularly amid

41 Adela Yarbro Collins, "Revelation, Book of," *ABD*: 695.

42 Collins, "Revelation, Book of," *ABD*: 695.

43 Wainwright, "Revelation, Book of," *DBI*: 390.

44 Larry V. Crutchfield, "Revelation in the New Testament Canon" in *A Bible Handbook to Revelation* Edited by Mal Couch (Grand Rapids: Kregel Publications, 2001), 31.

situations of chaos, exclusion, and ongoing oppression.[45] Since it has been written in the form of apocalyptic,[46] the message is usually expressed in vivid symbolism, sometimes of a bizarre kind.[47] As far as Revelation is concerned, apocalyptic has encouraged both passive detachments from the world and active subversion.[48]

Christopher Rowland identifying John's liberationist challenge to an imperial order argues that Revelation criticizes a political economy geared to the satisfaction of the fortunate minority at the centre of trade. It encourages suspicion of institutions, of our motives and the ongoing questioning of the character and extent of our involvement. It questions what is widely assumed to be reasonable and realistic by offering a different perspective on what we understand by rationality.[49] Richard Bauckham in a more evangelical vein champions Revelation's liberating impulses as anticipating a new world order to which the church bears prophetic witness even while persecuted by the beast.[50] W. M. Ramsay viewed that Revelation as a fine epistle to the seven churches in Asia; he says that in their conception they are strictly 'literary epistles,' deliberate and intentional imitations of a literary form that was already firmly established in Christian usage.[51] He further asserts that the Seven Letters spring from the sense of reality, the living vigorous instinct, from which the Christian spirit can never free itself,[52] what Ramsay mean here is that an apocalypse could not content John, it did not bring him close enough relation to his Churches, and, so as a second thought, he addressed the Seven representatives Churches one by

45 Harry O. Maier, *Apocalypse Recalled-The Book of Revelation after Christendom* (Minneapolis: Fortress Press, 2002), 8.

46 The apocalypticists were usually pessimistic about the present world. They despaired of man's efforts ever overcoming evil, and they looked to God to bring the victory (See Morris, *The Revelation of St. John*, 23).

47 Morris, *The Revelation of St. John*, 23.

48 Sweet, *Revelation*, 4.

49 Christopher Rowland, *Revelation* (London: Epworth, 1993), 135-36.

50 Maier, *Apocalypse Recalled*, 9.

51 W. M. Ramsay, *The Letters to the Seven Churches of Asia* (London: Hodder & Stoughton, 1904), 38-39.

52 Ramsay, *The Letters to the Seven Churches of Asia,* 37.

one.[53] Therefore, from the arguments made by various scholars, it can be summed up that Revelation is the book of prophecy, history, apocalyptic, vision, theology and the final destination of the Christian beliefs.

## 2.4. Historical Interpretation of Revelation

Even though Revelation contains many symbols that do not mean that each text has to be interpreted figuratively or allegorically. A literal interpretation can acknowledge and even celebrate the use of symbols. So, Dave Hagelberg uses the 'literal interpretation' in his book, meaning that whatever can be interpreted in a literal way should be interpreted in a literal way. And whatever does not make sense to interpret literally has to be given a figurative meaning.[54]

The crucial yet problematic task of the interpreter is to identify through careful exegesis and against the original historical background those texts which pertain respectively to past, present, and future.[55] Also, David Joy rightly pointed out by saying due to the lack of scientific and systematic approval, Revelation has been often misinterpreted and misled in various manners.[56] Because of this reason, scholars are proposing various schools of interpretation like Preterist, Historical, Idealist, Futurist, Spiritual, the Continuous-historical, Symbolic, and Moderate Futuristic.

Some principal methods of interpretation of Revelation are as follows:[57]

---

53 Ramsay, *The Letters to the Seven Churches of Asia*, 37.

54 Dave Hagelberg, *The Revelation of Jesus Christ Chapters 12-22* (Delhi: ISPCK, 2013), 14. Dave gave an example by saying the 'seven stars' which the Lord holds in His hand cannot be interpreted as literal stars, and Revelation 12:1 speaking about woman clothed with the sun is clearly full of figures of speech.

55 G. K. Beale, *The Book of Revelation: The New International Greek Testament Commentary* (Grand Rapids: Eersmans, 2013), 49.

56 Joy, *Revelation: A Post Colonial Viewpoint*, x.

57 The Rev. Canon Leon Morris, *The Revelation of St. John: An Introduction and Commentary* London: The Tyndale Press, 1969, 16-18; C. I. David Joy, *Revelation: A Post-Colonial View Point* Delhi: ISPCK, 2001, x-xi; Geoffrey W. Bromiley eds., *The International Standard Bible Encyclopaedia*. Volume 4, Grand Rapids: Eerdmans, 1988.

a. *The Preterist View*: This view starts with the situation of the church in the first century and ends there. It sees the book as arising out of the situation of the first Christians and is the outstanding merit of the preterist position. This method always mixes the message of the book of Revelation with the eschatological hope.
b. *The Historicist view*: This method tries to understand the book of Revelation as a purely historical standpoint. This view makes Revelation meaningful for this generation, at any rate in part. It is also curious that a book forecasting human history should largely ignore the world outside Western Europe.
c. *The Futurist view*: This method tries to understand Revelation as the prediction of things to come in the future. Some see the things described in the book with the end of the world, and as prefiguring those events which will usher in the second coming of the Lord Jesus Christ.
d. *The Idealist view*: This view asserts that the whole book is concerned with ideas and principles. It set out in poetic form certain theological conceptions. This resources its relevance for all periods of the church's history. In this view, the interpreters always try to locate themselves in one or the other stands in terms of understanding the message of the book of Revelation. This view narrates the non-historicity of the events and visions in the book of Revelation. As a result, the readers are guided to opt for a kind of allegorical interpretation.
e. *Spiritual view*: This method is closer to idealist but forces the readers to understand the message as the timeless truth.
f. *The Continuous-historical*: This method helps the readers to see the book of Revelation as literature which has serious implications in the present life situation of the church. The message to the seven churches can even speak to the present structure of the church.
g. *Symbolic*: Symbols used to help the readers to understand the meaning of the book of Revelation in a better way. Symbolism involved numbers, colour, animals, pictures,

images etc. Some of the symbols used in the book of Revelation are distinct to the book, at the same time some can be seen in the other books of the New Testament.

h. *Moderate Futuristic*: In this interpretation, Revelation is a prophecy of the denouncement of history as it concerns the church in the world.

Since this interpretative approaches includes fine variations in each of the methods, it helps to analyse, criticise and deeper understanding of the book. Therefore, these schools played a very crucial role in interpreting and understanding the book of Revelation. The historical development of the interpretation of Revelation can be highlighted as follows:

### *Early Interpretation to 300 C.E.*

The prevailing interpretation in early days was that of the Chiliasts (Millenialist), who regarded Rev. 20:1-6 as a prediction of Christ's coming reign on earth for a millennium, i.e., a thousand years. A widespread expectation was that the fall of Rome, symbolized by Babylon, would precede the millennium; and the connection between Antichrist and the beasts mentioned in the Apocalypse was much discussed.[58] To some extent, during the second and third century, Lange and Walvoord give a short history of how the book has been interpreted through the centuries. Walvoord notes: The second century like the first bears a sustained testimony to the premillennial character of the early church. Even the amillenarians claim no adherents whatever by name to their position in the second century except in the allegorizing school of interpretation which arose at the very close of the second century. He observed that in the third century premillennialism has emerged and those who mention this interpretation are: Cyprian (200-258 C.E.), Commodian (200-270 C.E.), Nepos (230-280 C.E.), Coracion (230-280 C.E.), Victorinus (240-303 C.E.), Methodius (250-311 C.E.), and Lactantius (240-330 C.E.).[59]

---

58 Wainwright, "Revelation, Book of" *DBI*: 390.

59 John F. Walvoord, *The Millennial Kingdom.* Ohio: Dunham, 1939. 120; Mal Couch ed., *A Bible Handbook to Revelation* Grand Rapids: Kregel Publications,

The spiritual interpretation of apocalypse was common in the early decades of the second century. Among the church fathers like Irenaeus, Justin Martyr, Clement are following the spiritual interpretation of apocalypse.[60] For example, Clement sees that the twenty-four elders in Revelation are a symbol of the equality of Jew and Gentile within the Christian Church.[61] Further, Bauckham also asserts that Revelation is an apocalypse, whose primary literary context is the tradition of Jewish and Christian apocalypses. Both in form and in content it is heavily indebted to this tradition.[62]

### *5th Century Reformation (400-1517 C.E.)*

Lange states that during the fifth century, people place the time of the Millennial Kingdom in the period intervening between the first coming of Christ in the flesh and the coming of anti-Christ. Jerome interprets Revelation allegorically denoting the Holy City as the present world. In the middle Ages, many people were certain that events recorded in Revelation would begin in the year 1000, assuming that the millennial kingdom began at the first coming of Christ. They modified their views and said the number 1000 is a symbolic number, denoting an indefinite period of time.[63]

### *The Reformation Era*

A new era of Apocalyptic exegesis begins in this period by the equation of 'Pope or the Papacy is Antichrist' was the cornerstone of

---

2001. 45-46.

60 Henry Barclay Swete, *The Apocalypse of St. John: The Greek Text with Introduction Notes and Indices* (Grand Rapids: Eerdmans, 1951), ccviiii.

61 Swete, *The Apocalypse of St. John*, ccviii.

62 Richard Bauckham, *The Climax of Prophecy: Studies on the Book of Revelation* (Edinburgh: T&T Clark, 1993), xi.

63 Couch, *A Bible Handbook to Revelation*, 46. He further states a historical-allegorical interpretation as Innocent III (1160-1216 C.E.) said that Islam was the Antichrist and Mohammed was the False Prophet. Pope Gregory IX (1145-1241 C.E.) said Frederick II, the Roman emperor was the beast of the abyss, and Joachim (1135-1262 C.E.) said Rome is the carnal church and the new Babylon. Dante (1265-1321 C.E.) said the Papacy was anti-Christian. Nicholas of Lyra (1270-1340 C.E.) regarded Revelation as a prophetic mirror of all history.

their interpretation.[64] Many people felt Revelation was a prophetic compendium of church history and that it was a settled issue to interpret papal Rome as the Antichrist. Luther arranged the fact of Revelation to fit his view of church history.[65] On the papal side, a counter-attempt to interpret the Apocalypse (Revelation) in the light of history was made by Nicolas of Lyra (1340). According to him, the millennium began with the founding of the Mendicant orders, which had bound Satan, as he thinks, for a considerable period of time. This is the so-called historical-allegorical interpretation.[66]

During the Reformation period, the new era of Apocalyptic exegesis begins. Each side in the great controversy found inspiration in this book. The reforming party inherited the method of Joachim and the Franciscans: the equation of 'the Pope, or the Papacy, is Antichrist' was the cornerstone of the Protestant attack, new methods arose, which at a later time found followers among the reformed. Their authors were Spaniards and members of the Society of Jesus. Francis Ribeira (1601), a professor at Salamanca, came to his task equipped with knowledge of both the Greek and Latin commentators of the patristic period, but with an open mind which refused to be bound by their exegesis. He took his stand on the principle that the Apocalyptist foresaw only the nearer future and the last things and offered no anticipations of intermediate history. Thus, he was able to relegate Anti-Christ to the time of the end, and though with the majority of the interpreters he identified Babylon with Rome, he could contend that the city which St. John saw upon the Beast was not, as some said, Rome under papal rule, but the degenerate Rome of a future age.[67]

### *The Seventeenth and Eighteenth Century*

During this period, the works of apocalyptic exposition flourished which also affects the interpretation of Revelation. Many people continued to see the Pope or Rome as the Anti-Christ. In England,

64 Swete, *The Apocalypse of St. John*, ccxiii.

65 Couch, *A Bible Handbook to Revelation*, 47.

66 Swete, *The Apocalypse of St. John*, ccxiii.

67 Swete, *The Apocalypse of St. John*, ccxiii-ccxiv.

Cambridge Mathematician Sir Isaac Newton (1642-1727 C.E.) and William Whiston (1667-1752 C.E.), found the fulfilment of John's prophecy from the days of Domitian to their own, and, the same system of interpretation was adopted by other scholars like Vitringa and Bengel.[68] At the end of the eighteenth century, a new approach of Revelation like a great poem or a drama was developed by Eichhorn that he broke up the text into acts and scenes-the drama of the progress and victory of the Christian faith.[69]

### *The Nineteenth Century*

The shifting of the approach of Revelation from the advocates of the continuously historical interpretation was turned into a more philosophical and theological interpretation. The study of Revelation brought a new interpretation and views of the apocalypse. Different methods have been used in interpreting the book. In the preterist view, the prophecies in the Apocalypse were fulfilled in the early days of the church.[70] The continuist or historical view sees Revelation as presenting a symbolic view of church history. This view was held by Martin Luther, Isaac Newton, and Elliot.[71]

### *Modern Period*

Modern scholars assumed that Revelation is the resistance movement of the Roman Imperialism. They give emphasis on the apocalyptic genre of Revelation that helps the reader to understand the reality of the audience. Further, the futuristic (eschatological) interpretation is emphasised and it focuses on the end of the world, a number of dates have been predicted for the end of the world, and, there are a number of difficulties with such interpretations.[72] At the same time, James Benedict argues that Revelation is considered as concerned

---

68 Swete, *The Apocalypse of St. John,* ccxiv.

69 Swete, *The Apocalypse of St. John,* ccxv.

70 Kepler, "Revelation, Book of," *DOB*: 850.

71 Couch, *A Bible Handbook to Revelation*, 47.

72 Gonzalez, *Revelation*, 9.

with both religious purity and with issues of social justice and economic exploitation.[73]

## 2.5. Apocalyptic Background in Revelation

Apocalyptic literature is always a response to a major crisis and it is intended for a group in crisis with the purpose of exhortation and/or consolation by means of divine authority which is seen in the book of Revelation.[74] The Book is in regard to its extraordinary complex nature and scope of a prophetic genre is acknowledged as an apocalyptic book. It is certainly a mysterious book full of curiosity and imagery, symbolic and allegorical. It is very different from other NT books in terms of its nature, genre, and characteristics.

### *The History of Apocalyptic*

The apocalyptic background could be traced back from the exilic period of Israelite history. The Assyrian destruction of Northern Israelite kingdom in 721 B.C.E. and the Babylonian destruction of Jerusalem Temple and the Southern Kingdom in 586 B.C.E. remark the historical importance of apocalyptic literature when the most community of Judahite had been exiled to Babylon.[75] During the exilic period, the Jewish apocalypticism makes its appearance and it changes Israel's view of the world and history. Information about God, history, Israel, and the world was now available through direct revelation to a seer (the one who sees visions).

According to the prevailing opinion, the great mass of apocalyptic literature came into being between 200 B.C.E. and 100 C.E. in the world of Semitic speaking (or at least strongly semantically influenced) Israel and Jewish Christianity.[76] But, if we look critically,

73 James Benedict, "The Great Whore Cast Down: Revelation 17-18 and the Imagery of Roman Conquest," *Spring* (2016), 39-48.

74 A. Peter Abir, *Conflict and Conquest: An Exegetico-Theological Study of Revelation 7-12* (Bangalore: Asian Trading Corporation, 1998), 5.

75 Frederick J. Murphy, *Apocalypticism in the Bible and Its World* (Grand Rapids: Baker Academic, 2012), 2.

76 Klaus Koch, *The Rediscovery of Apocalyptic* (London: SCM Press, 1972), 20.

it had its origin in the exilic period.[77] The war, destruction, and deportation which accompanied the Babylonian invasions during the early sixth century must have drastically reduced the population of Judah. The three major deportations in 597, 587/86 and 582 reduced the population of Judah and also represented the cream of Israelite society. During the decades that followed on the destruction of Jerusalem, the situation must have appeared hopeless to both the exiles and those remaining behind in Judah. In fact, this exile had a great effect on the society of the Jewish people. To relieve their despair and gives hope, King Cyrus permitting the Jews to return to their homeland and rebuild their temple in 515 B.C.E.[78] The religion and literature of the Jewish nation may be said to be the product of its history at every stage of its development, but this is particularly so with that expression of it in the inter-testamental period. The apocalyptic books constitute a record of these years, not in terms of a historical event, but in terms of the response of faith which the nation was called upon to make. The first, and greatest of all the Jewish apocalyptic writings, the Book of Daniel (the earliest apocalyptic book) was occasioned by the oppression of the Seleucid ruler, Antiochus IV Epiphanes (175-163 B.C.E.).[79] Furthermore, the book of Revelation was written during the reign of Roman Imperialism which portrays the Roman imperialistic drama and its resistance from the seer's (author) point of view.

## *Revelation in the Context of Apocalyptic*

Revelation is as mentioned earlier one of the backbones of apocalypticism. David E. Aune asserts that the proposed definition of the apocalyptic genre, with special reference to the Apocalypse of John is as follows: 1) *Form*: an apocalypse is a prose narrative, in autobiographical form, of revelatory message constitutes a literary climax, and framed by a narrative of the circumstances surrounding the revelatory experiences. 2) *Content*: the communication of a

77 Martin McNamara, *Intertestamental Literature* (USA: Michael Glazier Inc., 1983), 21-22.

78 Namara, *Intertestamental Literature*, 21-22.

79 D. S. Russell, *The Method and Message of Jewish Apocalyptic*, 16.

transcendent, often eschatological, perspective on human experience. 3) *Function*: (a) to legitimate the transcendent authorization of the message, (b) by meditating a new actualization of the original revelatory experience through literary devices, structures and imagery, which function to "conceal" the message which the text "reveals," so that (c) the recipients of the message will be encouraged to modify their cognitive and behavioural stance in conformity with transcendent perspective.[80] The author pretends to write about the Babylonians of the sixth century B.C.E., although the book really was written under the concerns the Romans at the end of the first century C.E. Therefore, the main address and focus on the book is the Roman Empire. The debate of whether Revelation is apocalyptic background or not among scholars still emerged, when James Kallas do not believe that Revelation is an apocalyptic book. He argued that Revelation is not an apocalyptic book because it has an attitude to suffering different from that of the apocalypses. He further discussed that in the apocalypses suffering comes from forces opposed to God, forces that God will eventually crash. Suffering is simply evil and is to be vigorously opposed.[81]

In following with this, Mazaferri asserts that 'Rev[elation] cannot be equated with apocalyptic in form. It lacks essential pseudonymity, while its written form is circumstantial...Its eschatology is Christian, with a modified temporal dualism and an optimistic view of the present. Its imminence is explicit and personal, not pseudo-prophetic, and conditional, not deterministic...Rev [elation] completely fails to qualify as a genuine apocalypse.'[82] While some scholars find difficult to see the genuine background of the apocalyptic feature in Revelation, Nickelsburg argued that Revelation is central to apocalyptic.[83] James

80 David E. Aune, *Apocalypticism, Prophecy, and Magic in Early Christianity*. Grand Rapids: Baker Academic, 2006, 60.

81 James Kallas, "The Apocalypse – an Apocalyptic Book?" *JBL*, Vol. Ixxxvi (1967): 69-80.

82 Christopher R. Smith, "*The Structure of the Book of Revelation in light of Apocalyptic Literary Conventions*" in *Novum Testamentum* XXXVI, Fasc. (4 Oct. 1994), 380.

83 George W. E. Nickelsburg, *The Apocalyptic Construction for Reality in 1 Enoch* (Collins & Charlesworth: 1991), 60.

Dunn also strongly believes that the apocalypse of John obviously stands firmly within the tradition of apocalyptic literature. He argued that Revelation is firmly in the tradition of apocalyptic literature in that it has clearly been born out of crises.[84] He further affirms that the main theological characteristics of apocalyptic literature are also present in Revelation. In supporting this, James Dunn further proposed an apocalyptic dualism which is used by Revelation like the struggles between the churches and pagan powers, Christ and Satan. The author of Revelation has no hope in this world; all his hopes are in heaven, and on the new heaven and the new earth.[85] He concluded that Revelation was true of apocalyptic genre.

In responding the arguments of the problems of apocalyptic genre in Revelation made by Hellholm, he argues that "by 'text' we can refer to a whole hierarchy of concepts of the generic nature. In this connection we have to ask the question in which ways certain texts are structurally similar to each other and characteristically different from others. In dealing with the simple signs such as predicates, I tried to show the importance of establishing a hierarchy of abstraction level such as "armchair, chair, seat, furniture." In dealing with such complex sign as 'genre' we have to proceed analogously, if genre analysis is to be successful at all. To my satisfaction, there seems to be an increasing agreement among linguists, literary critics, and even form critics that such a hierarchization is an absolute necessity. This is true, even if the terminology may differ and the theoretical reflection may have reached various levels of awareness."[86] David Aune affirms that the central message of an apocalypse coincides with a literary climax expresses in paradigmatic terms the proposal of Hellholm that the texts of the Apocalypse of John which the most embedded text at the highest communication level coincides with the highest grade of hierarchically arranged text sequences constitute

84 James D. G. Dunn, *Unity and Diversity in the New Testament* (London: SCM Press, 1977), 331-332.

85 Dunn, *Unity and Diversity in the New Testament,* 331-332.

86 David Hellhom, "The Problems of Apocalyptic Genre and the Apocalypse of John" Public Lecture delivered on February 18, 1982, at the Divinity School, The University of Chicago.

the central messages of these apocalypses.[87] Stephen also opines that apocalypse is rich in its use of symbols,[88] which is one of the common transmissions of Revelation. Therefore, despite the arguments of doubts of the apocalyptic genre in Revelation, the researcher affirms that the apocalyptic genre is definitely the background of Revelation.

## 2.6. Theology of Revelation

The theology of Revelation stands in the mainstream of first-century Christian thought since it had an apocalyptic background, apocalyptic theology plays an important role in the whole theology of Revelation. In the apocalyptic theology, the core of this kind of theology is a cosmic dualism, the belief that there are two opposing forces at work in the universe, one for evil (usually Satan and his demons) and one for good (usually God and the angels),[89] which mostly found in the book of Revelation. Apocalyptic theology also includes another kind of dualism, *a temporal dualism*. This dualism divides history into two ages, this age and the age to come.[90] Furthermore, the theology of Revelation was also enveloped by prophecy; Bauckham affirms that the task of the author is to proclaim the fulfilment of what God had revealed to the prophets of the past.[91] Revelation enriched with various literary genres like prophecy, vision, apocalyptic, symbols etc. To understand the theology of Revelation, it is important to know to the socio-historical milieu of the book. Revelation is an epistle to the Seven Churches in Asia, so also the theology is also depended upon the issues and condition of those churches.

### *Background of Asia Minor Churches*

The revelation was written to seven specific churches in the Roman province of Asia in the western part of what is called Asia Minor (now called Turkey). Ancient Asia Minor is a geographic region

---

87 Aune, *Apocalypticism, Prophecy, and Magic in Early Christianity*, 61.

88 Stephen S. Smalley, *The Revelation to John: A Commentary on the Greek Text of the Apocalypse* (Illinois: IVP Academic, 2005), 14.

89 Michael G. Gorman, *Reading Revelation Responsibly* (Eugene: Cascade Books, 2011), 15.

90 Gorman, *Reading Revelation Responsibly*, 16.

91 Bauckham, *The Theology of the Book of Revelation*, 4.

located in the south-western part of Asia comprising most of what is present-day Turkey. The earliest reference to the region comes from tablets of the Akkadian Dynasty (2334-2083 B.C.E) where it is known as "The Land of the Hatti" and was inhabited by the Hittites. The Hittites themselves referred to the land as "Assuwa" (or, earlier, Aswiya) which actually only designated the area around the delta of the river Cayster in Lydia but came to be applied to the entire region. Assuwa is considered the Bronze Age origin for the name 'Asia' as the Romans later designated the area. It was called, by the Greeks, "Anatolia" (literally, 'place of the rising sun', for those lands to the east of Greece).[92]

The name 'Asia Minor' (from the Greek 'Mikra Asia' - Little Asia) was first coined by the Christian historian Orosius (c. 375-418 C.E.) in his work Seven Books of History Against the Pagans in 400 C.E. to differentiate the main of Asia from that region which had been evangelized by the Apostle Paul (which included sites known from Paul's Epistles in the *Bible* such as Ephesus and Galicia). The Byzantine Empire of the 9th century C.E. referred to the region as "East Thema" which meant, simply, Eastern Administrative Division, and later sailors called it "The Levant" which meant 'the rising' or 'to rise' referring to how the land rose up out on the horizon of the sea. In the ancient world, Asia Minor was the seat of the kingdoms and cities of Thrace, Bythinia, Paphlagonia, Aeloia, Phrygia, Galicia, Pontus, Armenia, Urartu, Assyria, Cilicia, Pamphylia, Lycia, Pisidia, Lycaonia, Caria, Mysia, Ionia, Lydia, Troy.[93]

Under Roman rule, the land became stabilized; roads were built and the infrastructures of many of the cities improved. The coastal communities flourished and Ephesus, especially, enjoyed great prosperity until the rise of Christianity when 'earthly' advances in the region was neglected in anticipation of the Second Coming of Christ. The Byzantine Empire controlled the region after the fall of Rome in 476 C.E. and, after the rise of Islam, the later Byzantine Christians

92 *Joshua J. Mark*, 'Asia Minor' in *Ancient History Encyclopaedia*. Online Edition. Published on 4th May 2018. [Cited 13 July 2018]. Online: https://www.ancient.eu/Asia_Minor/.

93 Mark, 'Asia Minor' in *Ancient History Encyclopaedia.*

fought the Islamic Fatimids for the land until the coming of the Seljuq Turks in 1068 C.E. Turkish control increased in the region until 1299 C.E. when Asia Minor became part of the Ottoman Empire and, after its collapse, became Turkey. Although, apocalypses tend to be written during times of religious persecution, there is debate over how much Emperor Domitian (81-96 C.E.) actually cracked down. We find only one martyr mentioned in John's letters: Antipas in Pergamum. A careful reading of John's messages reveals that his primary concern for his churches is their accommodation to the surrounding Greco-Roman culture (where politics and religion are inseparable). The churches in Sardis and Laodicea, by yielding to the materialism around them, represent commercial accommodation; while some in the churches at Pergamum and Thyatira practice eating foods sacrificed to idols (2:14) or tolerate those who do (2:20), reflecting their adaptation to Roman civil religion. But, the 'synagogues of Satan' in Smyrna (2:9) and Philadelphia (3:9) seem like a different problem.[94]

Regarding the *social background*, the wealthy of that era were incredibly wealthy. Eating off silver plates was despised by the upper classes; gold plates were required. One emperor had a meal of peacock tongues. For a victory parade, one emperor clothed his entire army in silk, brought overland from China. In 18:11-17 the list of the great wealth of the upper classes of Rome at the time the book was written. Many were also extremely poor. Instead of a middle class, there was an enormous gap between the rich and the poor. Slavery was common. A slave was not considered human; he [sic] was property. In their *religious background*, Emperor Worship was common in those days; Christianity was recognized as a religion distinct from Judaism. Although, that might sound like it was positive for the Christians, it was not. Jews were excused from the otherwise mandatory worship of the emperor, but since the Christians were no longer considered a part of Judaism, they were no longer excused from emperor worship. Christians were considered atheists because they would not join in the religious practices of the Romans and did

94 Reta Halteman Finger, "*Conflict and Crisis in Asia Minor*" n.p. [cited 13 July 2018]. Online: https://eewc.com/conflict-crisis-asia-minor-revelation-2-3/.

not worship the Roman gods. Some churches and some Christians were being persecuted (1:9; 2:10, 13).[95] In the *political situation*, emperor worship was strongly recommended in the Roman province of Asia. Refusing to worship the emperor, to burn the incense and to say "Caesar is Lord," could easily result in death or banishment to a prison island, depending on the official's whim. The emperor Domitian enforced emperor worship, but there were no documents detailing how he enforced it. There had been persecution against Christians before the book was written (Antipas' martyrdom is mentioned in 2:13) and directly after it was written.[96] This clearly pictured the *status quo* of the Roman Empire in those days.

## Theology of Revelation-Theo-centric

The book of Revelation presents profound truths about God and His work, express in accords with its context, style, and purpose. Bauckham reminds us that John has no vocabulary equivalent to later Trinitarian talk of the divine nature which three persons share. But, it is impossible for us to do justice to what he says without speaking somehow of divine reality in which Jesus Christ and the Holy Spirit are included.[97] The whole book of Revelation centred to the attributes of God which manifest in various forms. The prominence of John gives to a 'Trinitarian' understanding of the divine in 1:4b-5a may justify our use of a Trinitarian structure for the major part of our account of the theology of Revelation. No such structure could be wholly satisfactory, but his one at least corresponds to a major feature of the theology of Revelation.[98]

## The Alpha and Omega

The phrase signifies the unique attributes of God's eternity. The idea was derived from Isaiah 44:6: "*I am the first and the last; besides me there is no god*" (NRSV). This designation encapsulates the understanding of the God of Israel as the sole Creator of all things

---

95 Hagelberg, *The Revelation of Jesus Christ to the Seven Churches and to us Chapters 1-11.* Delhi: ISPCK, 2013, 6-8).

96 Hagelberg, *The Revelation of Jesus Christ Chapter 1-11*, 6-8.

97 Bauckham, *The Theology of the Book of Revelation*, 25.

98 Bauckham, *The Theology of the Book of Revelation*, 25.

and the sovereign Lord of history.[99] Bauckham points out the unique importance of the designation-the Alpha and the Omega[100] by saying that God precedes all things, as their Creator, and he will bring all things to eschatological fulfilment. He is the origin and goal of all history. He has the first word, in creation, and the last word, in a new creation.[101] This title signifies the sovereign authority of God.

## *Judgment of God*

The political scenario of Revelation was enveloped with social injustice and political corruptness; therefore, Revelation pays attention to the final judgment. Justice is about exposing the truth of things. God's judgments are true in that they correspond to reality. They establish the truth, sweeping away the lies and illusions in which evil cloaks it. Thus, the themes of judgment and justice are closely connected with another central set of themes in Revelation: truth and deceit.[102] Elisabeth Schüssler Fiorenza rightly pointed out that in Revelation justice is understood as the conviction that each act brings about consequences which must be faced responsibly.[103]

---

99 Bauckham, *The Theology of the Book of Revelation*, 27. Here, Deutero-Isaiah magnificently expounds and asserts polemically against the idols of Babylon.

100 The form, 'the beginning and the end', had been used in the Greek philosophical tradition to indicate the eternity of the supreme God, and was taken over by Jewish writers, such as Josephus, who calls God 'the beginning and the end of all things' that John gives its two equivalents may be because he connects the former with the divine name. The Biblical name of God YHWH was sometimes vocalized Yāhôh and so transliterated into Greek (which has no consonant 'h') as IAW (Iota, Alpha, Omega). In the context of Jewish theological speculation about the divine name, the occurrence of the first and last letters of the Greek alphabet in this Greek form of the name could have suggested that the name itself contains the implication that God is the first and the last. (See Bauckham, *The Theology of the Book of Revelation*, 27-28.]

101 Bauckham, *The Theology of the Book of Revelation*, 27.

102 Richard Bauckham, "Judgment in the Book of Revelation" *Ex auditu*, 20 (2004), 1-24.

103 E. Schüssler Fiorenza, *Revelation: Vision of a Just World* (Edinburgh: T&T Clark, 1993), 95.

## 2.7. Conclusion

The above research of the milieu of the book of Revelation shows that Revelation is very much complex and controversial because of its various literary genres; it's a unique style of writing and the mixture of prophecy, apocalyptic and epistles. And, it is important to note that the book contains not only of religious purities, but also political, economic issues and social injustices. By looking at the context of the community, the writer clearly portrays the Revelations' contemporary, despite having a corrupt unjust socio-political background, under such circumstances the early Christians were exploited, oppressed and persecuted. In such a critical condition, the book of Revelation gives hope and brings justice to an unjust socio-economic structure of the Roman Empire.

Chapter 3

# The Identity of Babylon and Economic Issues in Revelation 18

## 3.1. Introduction

This chapter deals with the biblical symbolism and its meaning to identify the nature and identity of Babylon, it also deals with the scholars' debate about the identity of Babylon whether Rome or Jerusalem. The quest of Babylon's identity gives us information that helps to understand the issue in Revelation 18. The study also allocates the background of the Roman Empire along with the unjust economic issues found in Revelation 18 which portrays the real identity of Babylon.

## 3.2. Meaning of Symbol/Symbolism

Revelation used Babylon in a symbolic language. Symbolic language is one of the common transmissions in the early centuries especially in the apocalyptic literature as found in Revelation. Ernest Johnson described the word "symbol" as it is derived from the Greek verb, *symballō*. It is perhaps true that the noun, "symbolon," takes its meaning as a sign by which one knows or infers something, from the extended sense of *symballō*, to compare hence to conjecture or to infer. In the medical world, *symbolon* meant a symptom or distinctive mark. Yet the deeper significance of the word, 'symbol," lies in the more original sense of the verb, "to bring together."[104] He further mentioned that symbol translates a human situation into cosmological terms and vice versa; more precisely, it reveals the continuity between the structures of human existence and cosmic structures. A symbol is a representative of a transcendent and invisible reality by means of an image borrowed from the sensuous and visible. Symbol differs from metaphor and analogy by the fact that the reality to which it points is not available for rational recognition. Thus, a symbol points to a hidden and mysterious reality and is held to be analogous to it. Yet the presence of such analogy is given in the experience of the reality and results from intuitive insight. Symbol sometimes belongs to the realm of words and communication. Symbolism takes form under human discourse as it is confronted by a revelatory depth in reality. Unlike images and signs, symbols participate in the sacred reality which they represent and are the accompaniment of all revelation. In ancient times, People express their religious belief by symbols. Countless symbols made over a period of 4,000 years or more have been found on cylinder seals, clay tablets, jar handles etc. which signifies Symbol was familiar and common in Near East. The Canaanite made a myriad of gods in the form of men, like the storm god Baal or Hadad; winged lions and griffins, which represented the aggressive power of Babylon and so on.[105]

Furthermore, a symbol is more than a sign since the latter does not imply a representation of the signified; it brings together a linguistic dimension and another dimension which is of a non-linguistic nature.[106] A sociologist has stressed that symbols must be generally accepted by a group, community, or society in order to persist and that there must be a certain consensus on their meaning require a certain authority. Religious symbols, for instance, require a

---

104 F. Ernest Johnson, ed., *Religious Symbolism* London: The Institute for Religious and Social Studies, 1955. 3; Eric C. Rust, "Symbol" *MDB:* 865; J. A. Ross Mackenzie, HBD: 1003-1007.

105 Johnson, ed., *Religious Symbolism,* 1003-1007.

106 Alan M. Olson, ed., *Myth, Symbol and Reality* (London: University of Notre Dame Press, 1980), 42.

religious legitimation supported by charismatic or other authority.[107] A symbol is not simply an externally visible imagination; rather it is an outcome of the psycho inner thoughts. Mircea Eliade asserts that Symbol reveals a certain aspect of reality-the deepest aspects which defy any other means of knowledge.[108]

Albert D'Souza also defines symbol as a symbol is a term whose significant use or purpose is expressive. Diel also argues that the symbol is a vehicle at once universal and particular. It also relates it to a definite period of history. Hindu Philosopher Ananda K. Coomaraswamy also said that symbolism is the art of thinking in images. E. Boring summarized an approach to the interpretation of symbols in the Apocalypse that has come to be widely held. He further states that symbols are not to be decoded into propositional language that refers to objective realities, but are to be left as non-objectifying pictorial language that only point to ultimate reality but cannot describe it, since it transcends our finite minds and cognitive categories of language.[109]

The identification of symbols in Revelation with first-century historical realities is partly correct but does not exclude applications of the symbols to historical realities in subsequent generations.[110] Revelation's language does not adhere to the laws of logical propositional language and is non-inferential because John attempts to communicate the reality of God's transcendent world by words bounded by space and time. Hence, the language of Revelation is not diachronic but synchronic, and it employs pictorial language which uses myth as the vehicle of truth.[111] Therefore, symbolism plays a crucial role in the book of Revelation. This research pursued

---

107 Olson, *Myth, Symbol and Reality*, 46.

108 Mircea Eliade, *Images and Symbols- Studies in Religious Symbolism* (New York: Search Book, 1969), 12.

109 Albert D'Souza, *Studies in Religious Imagination and Symbolism.* New Delhi: A Mittal Publication, 2005, 14; J. E. Cirlot, *A Dictionary of Symbols.* New York: Routledge & Kegan, 1962, xvi

110 Beale, *The Book of Revelation: A Commentary on the Greek Text* (Grand Rapids: Eerdmans, 1999), 65.

111 Beale, *The Book of Revelation*, 65.

the symbolic interpretation of Babylon in Revelation and brings out how Babylon in Revelation symbolises the Roman Empire.

### 3.3. Terminology and Historical Babylon

Babylon went by a variety of names in antiquity. The earliest form of the toponym appears to have been *babil(a),* which has neither Sumerian or Akkadian origin. But, it appears to have given rise to an Akkadian form, created through popular etymology *bab-ilim*, "Gate of God" and a Sumerian equivalent, *ka-dingirra*, also meaning "Gate of God." The later plural Akkadian form, *ba-bilani*, "Gate of Gods" became '*babulon*' in Greek, resulting in the modern name "Babylon."[112] With regards to the OT concept of Babylon, Bill T. Arnold remarks that because of its international and cultural significance and its role later in destroying Jerusalem and deporting large positions of its citizens, Babylon came to carry theological significance in the Bible even beyond its obvious historical importance. The city itself came to symbolized ungodly power. Steven Friesen opines that the NT traditions treat Babylon as a significant marker in the history of Israel and as a metaphor for the experience of the churches in the Roman Empire. Historical Babylon is a city in southern Mesopotamia, located on a branch of the Euphrates, 59 miles (90 km) southwest of Baghdad. Babylon rose to prominence early in the 2nd Millennium B.C.E. as the region experienced significant socio-political changes, and became the capital of important political entities throughout various periods of ancient Near Eastern history, playing a significant role in Israel history and ideology.[113] Saggs remarks that the reign of Nebuchadnezzar was a time of great building activity in Babylonia; the empire had reached its peak because of their wise and great king Nebuchadnezzar.[114]

When Nabopolassar (625-605 B.C.E.) became king of Babylon, he founded the Babylonian empire more stable and well-structured. His son, Nebuchadnezzar II, invaded and took over the provinces of

112 Bill T. Arnold, "Babylon, OT," *NIDB*: 376-380.

113 Arnold, "Babylon, OT," *NIDB*: 376-380.

114 H. W. F. Saggs, *The Greatness that was Babylon* (New York: Hawthorn Books, 1962), 141.

the Assyrian Empire from the Mediterranean Sea to the Persian Gulf. Like the Assyrian style, the Babylonian king began then to appear annually with his army to collect tribute and to conquer and punish recalcitrant cities such as Jerusalem in 597 and 586 B.C.E. During the reign of the last ruler of Babylonia, Nabonidus (555-539 B.C.E.), Persian emperor Cyrus moved into the capital without encountering resistance and this was the end of Babylonian Sovereignty, but that the spirit of the country was not yet dead is brought home by the fact that two later pretenders to the Babylonian throne took the magic name of Nebuchadnezzar.[115] The socio-economic political condition was well structured and we may find many similarities in socio-political and economic dimensions in the Roman Empire in NT.

## 3.4. The Quest of the Identity of Babylon in Revelation

The name Babylon certainly brings to mind ideas of the worldwide rule, the destruction of the temple, the exile, and vast economic control, by taking this approach, these themes are much appropriate and insufficient to explain its use in Revelation. By connecting this name to the descriptions of Babylon in Isaiah, Jeremiah, Ezekiel, and Daniel, Revelation recalls the idolatry and pride of that ancient city, a city whose ruler saw themselves and their gods as supreme. The name 'Babylon' is a guarantee that no 'Babylon' –ancient or modern is able to stand before the judgment of God; consequently, the use of this particular title brings encouragement to those who hear and read Revelation. Regardless of Babylon's outward strength and prosperity, the reality is that Babylon will be fallen.[116]

In the book of Revelation, Babylon refers to the great as a city which seduced kings and those who dwell on earth to imbibe the wine of her sexual immorality (καὶ ἐμεθύσθησαν οἱ κατοικοῦντες τὴν γῆν ἐκ τοῦ οἴνου τῆς πορνείας αὐτῆς Rev 17:2).[117] Gregory states that the title "Babylon" should not be explained simply by making a connection with Rome. But, it should be noted that Revelation

115 Leo Oppenheim, *Ancient Mesopotamia* Revised Edition; Chicago: University of Chicago Press, 1977, 161-163.

116 Peter F. Gregory, "Its End Is Destruction: Babylon the Great in the Book of Revelation," *CTQ*, 73 No. (2 April 2009),137-153.

117 Gregory, "Its end is Destruction...," 137-153.

picks up most particularly the language of Babylon's fall.[118] Robert Mounce also describes the reason for using Babylon as the reader will know what God did to first Babylon and be quick to recognize that in giving Rome that title he will once again carry out his judgment on the city.[119] Further, the Anchor Bible Dictionary describes the connection between ancient Babylon and Babylon the Great (Rome) as – like Babylon, Rome ruled the kings of the earth (14:8; 17:1-2, 15, 18), was a centre of world trade (14:8; 18:2-3), revealed in luxury (18:7, 11-17, 22-23), was a persecutor of God's covenant people (1718:24), and was destined to fall (18:2).[120] Meanwhile, scholars like G. K. Beale, J. Christian Wilson assumed that symbolic Babylon was Jerusalem while J. J. Collins and Hunzinger assert that Babylon was Rome. He argues that those preferring a pre-70 C.E. date for Revelation regard "Babylon" as a symbolic name for apostate Jerusalem, but John's use of the name may be the strongest internal evidence for a post 70 date. Collins also assumed that Babylon in Revelation refers to Rome in Jewish literature after 70 C.E. and roughly contemporary with the Apocalypse (Revelation). Hunzinger also asserts that Jewish commentators called Rome "Babylon" because the Roman armies destroyed Jerusalem and its temple in 70 C.E., just as Babylon had done in the sixth century B.C.E. He further suggests that this use of the name probably influenced John, as did other Jewish traditions. Jewish writings might have referred to Rome as Babylon before 70 C.E. merely out of a belief that Jews were still in exile, even though they were living in the Promised Land because they were oppressed by a foreign power, yet still expected to occur when Israel's exile was completely ended.[121] J. Christian Wilson argues that in Jewish literature prior to 70 C.E. (OT, LXX, DSS, Pseudepigrapha) Babylon was associated primarily with the exile and only rarely linked with Jerusalem's destruction, and, in Revelation, "Babylon" is never linked with Jerusalem's destruction but represent

118 Gregory, "Its end is Destruction…," 152.

119 Robert H. Mounce, *The Book of Revelation* (First Revised Edition; Grand Rapids: Eerdmans, 1998), 325.

120 Duane F. Watson, "Babylon", *ABD*: 566.

121 Beale, *The Book of Revelation,* 18; A. Y. Collins, *Crisis and Catharsis: The Power of the Apocalypse.* Philadelphia: Westminster, 1984;

only the place in which the saints live in exile. Therefore, Wilson concludes that Revelation was written prior to 70 C.E.[122]

Despite some disputes of Babylon as Rome among the scholars, most commentators agree that Babylon as Rome in Revelation, among which Richard Bauckham opines that Babylon is the city of Rome and in particular the city of Rome as a corrupting influence on the people of the empire, rides on the back of Roman military power.[123] In following this, David Joy also remarks about the symbolic usage of Babylon as Rome as Babylon stands as a symbol of crime and shame in the history of the world, so also Rome that they were most powerful and influential... all the metaphors are clearly referring to the processor state of idolatry, misuse of power, sexual abuse and disorder, corruption and dehumanising activities of the Roman Emperors.[124] From the above discussion, it is presumable that the debate of Babylon's identity was a controversial issue among scholars.

## 3.5. Babylon in Revelation: Rome or Jerusalem?

The debate of whether Babylon is Rome or Jerusalem brings an informative and challenging discussion. The Babylon of Revelation 17-18 has been interpreted as imperial Rome since antiquity, but some scholars have rejected such a solution in recent centuries and have held that Babylon instead should be Jerusalem rather than Rome. NT scholars are discussing and debating about whether Babylon in Revelation is Rome or Jerusalem. Both the arguments defend their stance purposefully.

A. J. Beagley proposed both the arguments by saying Babylon as a reference to pagan Rome, the city. While the beast on which she rides represents the Roman Empire on which the city depends. The further explanation that the woman is the great city that rules over

---

122 J. C. Wilson, "Babylon as Cipher for Rome and Dating of Early Jewish and Early Christian Documents." Unpublished paper read at the 1994 Annual Meeting of the Society of Biblical Literature quoted by Beale in *The Book of Revelation,* 19.

123 Richard Bauckham, *The Climax of Prophecy-Studies on the Book of Revelation* (Edinburgh: T&T Clark, 1993), 343-345.

124 Joy, *Revelation-A Post-Colonial View Point,* 77-79.

the kings of the earth (17:18) is alleged to point to Rome's political dominance, the lament of the merchants over her fall because no one buys their cargoes any more (Rev 18:11) to her position as a trading power. In contrast to this, he also proposed arguments of Babylon as Jerusalem; Jerusalem was a substantial importer of just the kinds of goods that are named in Revelation 18:12-13. Much of what is said about "Babylon" applies better to Jerusalem than it does to Rome.[125]

G. Biguzzi also studied about the identity of Babylon in Revelation; he proposed the two hypotheses as Anti-Jewish interpretation and Anti-Roman interpretation. He listed both the views in making various points as follows:[126]

### *Reasons against the Anti-Roman Hypothesis*

i) The alleged anti-Roman attitude of Rev is belied by the pro-Roman stance of all other political NT statements (Rom 13:1; 1Pet 2:13-14; 1 Tim 2:1-4 etc). In the case that Revelation was an anti-Roman libel; no historical 1st Century event could explain such a change of attitude towards Rome from the Christian side.

ii) The anti-Roman interpretation is based on the allegedly anti-Christian persecution of Domitian and his alleged promotion of the emperor cult, but the only persecution of Christians in the 1st Century was that unleashed by Nero in the city of Rome alone, while the number of temples dedicated to the imperial cult was no higher under Domitian than under both his predecessors and successors.

iii) Babylon is labelled as "harlot," but only (Israel or) Jerusalem, who is the bride of Yahweh, can become a harlot, as attested in the OT, not Rome.

iv) The head wounded by the sword (13, 14) or the Beast that "was, but is not" (17, 8) cannot be identified with the Nero *redivivus* and *redux*, because such legend is posterior to the emperor Trajan.

125 A. J. Beagley, "Babylon" *DLNTD*: 111-112.

126 G. Biguzzi, "Is the Babylon of Revelation Rome or Jerusalem?" *Biblica* Vol. 87 No. 3 (2006), 371-386.

v) Rev 11 speaks of "the Great City" (v. 8), exactly as Rev 17-18 does for Babylon. But, the Great City in Rev 11 is without any doubt Jerusalem, since it is also called "the holy city" (v. 2), since its sanctuary (ό ναός) and "courtyard of the Gentiles" (ή αὐλὴν ή ἔξωθεν) are mentioned (vv. 1-2), and since in that Great City "their Lord was crucified." As an inevitable consequence, Babylon/ "the Great City" is the same as Jerusalem/ "the Great City."

### *Reasons against Anti-Jerusalem Hypothesis*

i) Prostitution. It is, of course, true that Israel in the OT is represented as Adonay's bride and is charged with harlotry, but prostitution (πορνεια) is not to be hurriedly identified with adultery (μοιχεία), because an unmarried woman can also be a harlot. Furthermore, Tyre (Isa 23:17) and Nineveh (Nah 3:4) is accused of harlotry as well. Finally, whereas in the OT Jerusalem is accused of letting itself be corrupted by the idolatry of the nations, in Rev, on the contrary, Babylon is corrupting them with its own idolatry.
ii) The two different idolatries. Rev 9:20-21 speaks of the idolatry of the (many) idols and demons, and Rev 13ff speaks of the particular idolatry of the Beast (with only one cultic image, the εικών of the Beast; 13:14, and passim). The first idolatry is struck by the plagues of the trumpets and the second by the plagues of the bowls. While two such distinguishable idolatries would hardly correspond to any historic or even symbolic datum in the Jerusalem of the First Century C.E., they are easily identified with the traditional idolatry of the Roman-Hellenistic pantheon, which was present in every town and village, and the emperor cult, whose native land and actual centre was exactly in Asia Minor.

The major difficulty against the anti-Jewish interpretation comes from the dating of Rev. According to Corsini, Beagley, and Lupieri, Revelation was written after the destruction of Jerusalem (70 C.E.) and, according to Josephine Massyngberde Ford, after 66

C.E. Yet, both during the revolt and after its destruction, Jerusalem was furiously fighting or enraged against Rome. Consequently, it is inconceivable that its religious power was in "monstrous alliance" with the Roman political establishment.

Furthermore, the anti-Roman hypothesis suggests that Babylon is 'drunk with the blood of the saints' according to Rev 17:6, and Jerusalem, not Rome, persecuted the OT prophets and Jesus' disciples; the perfect symmetry between Rev 17-18 and Rev 21 suggests that Babylon (Rev 17-18) is the symmetrical opposite of the holy Jerusalem (Rev 21) and, as such, is the terrestrial and corrupt Jerusalem; the seven mountains (ἑπτα ορη) of Rev 17:9 cannot be interpreted as the seven hills of Rome, because Rome's hills are called λοφοι by Greek writers, not ορ, and Rome is always called επταλφος, never ἑπτάορος; the seven kings of Rev 17:9-10 cannot be interpreted as seven of the Roman emperors, because the counting is unsuccessful, either beginning from Julius Caesar, or Augustus, or Caligula, or Nero etc., and even omitting one, or two, or all the three emperors of the year 69 C.E., Galba, Otho, and Vitellius[127] which signifies Babylon as Rome.

Biguzzi continues to describe that the major argument of the anti-Jewish interpretation is not invincible. In fact, the Great City spoken of in Rev 11 is divided into two fronts. On one side there is the sanctuary, the worshipers in it, and the two Witnesses of the Crucified Lord, who all without any doubt are to be interpreted as the Christians. On the other, there are the "pagans," who will trample over the holy city (v. 2) and rejoice for the murder of the two Witnesses (vv. 9-10).[128] As a consequence, Jerusalem in Rev 11 is a symbol partly of the Christians and part of the nations, but never and nowhere of the Jews. Secondly, the city trampled on by the pagans, and scenario of the story of the two Witnesses, oscillates from urban (vv. 1-2) to universal dimension ("men from the peoples and tribes and tongues and nations gaze etc.," v. 9: "all the inhabitants of the earth rejoice etc.," v. 10b), and back again to urban (v. 13). All this

127 Biguzzi, "Is the Babylon of Revelation Rome or Jerusalem?" 377.

128 Biguzzi, "Is the Babylon of Revelation Rome or Jerusalem?" 382.

entails that the Jerusalem of Rev 11 is a symbol of the whole world, where the messianic and anti-messianic forces come to collide.[129]

Therefore, after discussing and going through the pros and cons of the two interpretations and scholar's assumptions and hypothesis, it can be concluded that the traditional understanding of Babylon as Rome is more acceptable than Jerusalem. This research would also further proceeds and follows the pattern of Rome as a symbolism of Babylon.

## 3.6. Background of Roman Empire

The socio-political and economic background of Roman Empire portrays the situation and context of Revelation and also the community. Therefore, let us briefly highlight the political and social dimension of the Roman Empire.

### *Political Background*

The Roman Empire was, in fact, a military dictatorship which was supported by the army, the emperor the commander-in-chief took on all the powers shares up to then between the Senate (representing *latifundista* patrician family) and the people (representing the Roman citizens). The Roman Empire control the province of Asia in 133 B.C.E. within the larger geographic region of Asia Minor, it is noteworthy that this was achieved not by force, but by the granting of territory by King Attalus of Pergamum to Rome. The only real resistance to Roman rule came with the temporary expulsion between 88 and 86 B.C.E. of Roman authority from Asia by a local king supported by both the elite and poorer classes. Augustus' victory put an end to the war between the Roman elite in 31 B.C.E. When coming to the fourth century B.C.E., the Roman Empire was then at its peak, the city of Rome had gradually conquered all of Italy, then the whole of the Mediterranean basin.[130] The emperor encouraged more and more the development of a business bourgeoisie, the knights, who occupied the higher

---

129 Biguzzi, "Is the Babylon of Revelation Rome or Jerusalem?" 383.

130 Howard-Brook, *Unveiling Empire,* 92; Michel Clevenot, *Materialistic Approaches to the Bible* Translated by William J. Nottingham, New York: Orbis Book, 1985. 53.

functions of the administration and participated directly in the imperialist exploitation through the great colonial trade and through the furnishing of military supplies. The state was a power of coercion benefiting the ruling class of landowners who were deprived of the means of production. Gradually the bureaucracy took away all the power of the deliberating assemblies, especially of the Senate. The public treasury (*aerarium*) was neglected in favour of the Emperor's treasury (*fiscus*). The emperor was the greatest landholder and handled all the public expenditures.[131] In the same meaning, the power of the Republic was slowly handed to the elite group and the sole authority was at the hand of Roman Emperors.

The Roman Empire was very hierarchical with a huge gap between the wealthy, powerful elite and the rest of the population. Kautsky observes that elites, especially but nor exclusively elite males, conventionally occupied roles such as warrior, ruler, judge, administrator, patron, and priest in imperial and civic cults. Elite values and practices involved euergetism (acts of civic benefaction and patronage), the quest for public honour, the superiority of their own social status and race, and the conspicuous consumption and display of wealth through education, housing, clothing food, and acts of patronage.[132] A huge socio-economic gap separated the wealthy and powerful from skilled and unskilled urban workers, rural peasants working small landholdings, day labourers, and slaves. And, elites also controlled much urban production, intercity trade and commerce, and urban-rural interactions involving trade, investment, and banking.[133]

### *Social Background*

Roman society was built on a pyramid of patron-client relationships. Rome had long defined its citizens and strangers by rank and status with senators, equities, plebs, including freedmen, as well as foreigners and encouraged the former groups by means of privileges

131 Clevenot, *Materialistic Approaches to the Bible,* 56.

132 Warren Carter, *John and Empire: Initial Exploration* (London: T&T Clark, 2008), 53-4.

133 Carter, *John and Empire,* 53.

to be proud of whom they were. The senators were the highest class and were social equals of the emperor.[134] A person of higher standing (patron) could offer financial assistance or legal protection (patronage) to a person of lower standing (client). By accepting assistance, the client was obligated to offer respect and loyalty to the patron.[135] Due to the oppressive dominion of the ruling elite group, as for the oppressed classes of ruined peasants, citizens, and the unemployed, the wanderers, foreigners, and slaves, they had no earthly hope.[136] The ruling class, which constituted about five percent of the population, had a total monopoly on political and military power and this group lived from the produce they took from the majority (i.e., ninety percent) of the population. The rulers forced the peasants to produce more than they would have needed for their subsistence so that they could take the 'surplus' in the form of tax, rent or tribute to support themselves and their servants. While the rulers, their servants, and retainers lived mainly in the fortified cities, the peasant producers lived and worked in the countryside.[137]

In relation to the social life, the emperors are the major responsibilities of the authority, while the Senate was the titular controllers of economic policy with their ability to levy taxes and authorize payments, the emperor had they trumped in more ways than just controlling how they voted. He was the direct Governor of all the key provinces of the Empire, called imperial provinces, both those which were militarily vital and those which formed the core of the imperial revenue stream.[138] Since the emperor had the highest authority, whatever the decision he had made should be accomplished which also had a deep impact on the society.

---

134 Peter Oakes ed., *Rome in the Bible and the Early Church* (UK: Paternoster Press, 2002), 76.

135 Howard Brook, *Unveiling Empire*, 95.

136 Clevenot, *Materialistic Approaches to the Bible*, 57.

137 Sam P. Matthew, *Temple-Criticism in Mark's Gospel* (Delhi: ISPCK, 1999), 77.

138 Barbara Levick, *The Government of Roman Empire* (London: Routledge, 2000), 126.

## *The Oppressive Socio-Economic System of Rome*

While discussing the social milieu of the Roman society, it has to be noted that the economic structure of the first-century Roman Empire produced a number of socio-economic tensions. The first was the tension between city and country. Within the city, there was tension between the elite, who owned and controlled the food supplies, and the poor majority, who were dependent on food aid. In the rural areas, there was tension between the tenanted peasants and the owners of the large estates and between the peasants and those representatives of the empire-Rome and the provinces, which benefited the provincial elite and impoverished the majority.[139] The economic imbalance of urban and rural becomes a source of deep disaffection.

## *Economic Background*

The first century Palestine was an agrarian society with a population mostly of peasant farmers eking out subsistence from the land either as free peasants, tenants, day labourers or agricultural slaves.[140] Because of this agrarian economy, addressing an analysis of the territorial situation and taxation will help us about the economic condition of that time. Rostovtzeff observes the economic condition of the Roman empire as Judea, Samaria, and still more Galilee are studded with hundreds of villages inhabited by peasants, above whom stands a native aristocracy of large landowners, who are patrons of the villages...still more opulent are the officials of the kings and tetrarchs themselves and their families. Lastly, we find estates of the Roman Emperor himself and the imperial family, and even a Roman military colony established by Vespasian at Emmaus after the Jewish war.[141]

Revelation locates Rome's illicit economic activity within the larger context of Rome's imperial rule secured by military power and religious practices, the imperial cult presents Roman political power as sanctioned by the gods and fosters submissive compliance,

139 Howard Brook, *Unveiling Empire*, 101.

140 Matthew, *Temple-Criticism in Mark's Gospel*, 88.

141 M. Rostovtzeff, *The Social and Economic History of the Roman Empire*, 2 Vols. (Second Edition; Oxford: Clarendon Press, 1979), 270.

and economic activity means participation in this political-military-religious power.[142] Revelation 18 emphasizes the interconnections of economic extravagance with the idolatrous self-glorification of religious observance and the political control of an eternal empire; economic oppression is embedded in the empire's political-religious control and sustained by its military viciousness.[143] In addition to this, a small group of (about 1-3%) the population so-called ruling elites controlled much of the power, wealth and status. And the rest of 97% experience degrees of powerlessness and poverty. C. R. Whittaker observes that the term "poor" in Roman status terms usually meant anyone, not of the ruling orders. While most were poor, there were gradations of poverty. Estimates of preindustrial cities identify 4-8 percent as incapable of earning a living, 20 percent in permanent crisis, and 30-40 percent (artisans, shopkeepers, officials) who temporarily fall below subsistence levels for at least short periods. In a recent study, Steven Friesen estimates, while conceding the provisional nature of the numbers, that 28 percent lived below subsistence level, 40 percent at subsistence, and 22 percent stable near subsistence, 7 percent with a moderate surplus, and elites constituted the remaining 3 percent. Furthermore, Elite households gained necessary cash flow from land, loan interest and repayment, trade, inheritances, and rents from houses, warehouses, apartments, and shops. In terms of allegiance to the empire, Peter Brunt concludes that "We can never know how deeply that loyalty penetrated the masses," though clearly, they were not immune from the continual visual and system displays of Roman power. Economic control was exercised through ownership of resources, notably land and labour (slaves, day labourers, tenants, tenant farmers etc), property and trade. Kautsky argues that Rome's empire exhibits some commercialization in that elites not only took peasants production through taxation, as traditional agrarian empires do but also controlled the land itself.[144]

142 Warren Carter, *The Roman Empire and the New Testament* (Nashville: Abingdon Press, 2006), 105-6.

143 Carter, *The Roman Empire and the New Testament*, 106.

144 Carter, *John and Empire*, 53; C. R. Whittaker, "The Poor" in *The Romans* Edited by Andrea Giardina. Chicago: University of Chicago Press, 1993, 272-

## 3.7. Unjust Economic Issues in Revelation 18

Revelation focuses its attack not Babylon's architecture or physical layout, but on its trade and alliances. The luxurious life and love of money bring a forged corruption in the society, misuse of power and economic authority found in the Roman Empire. Some of the unjust economic issues have been described below.

### *Babylon as Economic Exploiter*

Rome was a World Trade Centre, an economic engine of the world, controlling vast territories and peoples and amazing great wealth through its shipping and trade.[145] Under the empire, we see the economic changes both the inequality and reciprocity that were embedded in the Roman Empire. Economic exchanges between centre and periphery, metropolis and the margins, imperial and colonial as doomed.[146] The economic structure of the Roman Empire produced a number of social tensions. First was the tension between city and country. Within the city, there was tension between the elite, who owned and control the food supplies, and the poor majority, who were dependent on food aid. In the rural areas, there was tension between the tenanted peasants and the owners of the large estates. And between the peasants and those representatives of the empire who taxed them. There was also tension between the centre of the empire- Rome and the provinces, which benefited the provincial elite and impoverished the majority.[147] Thus, while some

---

299; Steven Friesen, "Poverty in Pauline Studies: Beyond the so-called New Concensus," *JSNT* 26 (2004): 323-61; C. R. Whittaker, *Land, City and Trade in the Roman Empire.* Aldershot: Variorum, 1993; Helen Parkins eds., *Roman Urbanism: Beyond the Consumer City.* London: Routledge, 1997. 83-111; Peter Brunt, *Roman Imperial Themes.* Oxford: Claredon, 1990. 227; John Kautsky, *The Politics of Aristocratic Empires.* Chapel Hill: University of North Carolina Press, 1982. 159-82).

145 Barbara R. Rossing, *The Choice of Between Two Cities-Whore, Bride and Empire in the Apocalypse* (USA: Trinity Press International, 1999), 117.

146 Rohun Park, "Revelation for Sale: An Intercultural Reading of Revelation 18 from an East Asian Perspective," *The Bible and Critical Theory*, Vol. 4, No. 2, (Monarch University Press, 2008), 251.

147 Howard-Brook, *Unveiling Empire*...171.

praised Rome for its prosperity created by conquest and trade, for others this was a source of deep disaffection.

The list of cargoes was only available to the elite Roman society. These same goods are listed again as commodities imported by Babylon (18:2), and as the commodities destroyed in the fall of the city of Babylon (18:16). Revelation 18 contains a concentrated depiction of the affluence of Babylon. This affluence comes to naught in Babylon's fall. Those who had benefited from the city-the kings, the traders, and the seafarers- are envisioned as mourning the loss of the city.[148] Revelation 18 demonstrates a clear awareness of how the economy of Babylon operated and whom it benefited.

The wealth of Rome is beyond measured by comparing those contemporaries since her foreign economic policy was a success in various ways. By the second century a considerable amount of goods from the empire-expensive glass and drinking cups of silver, plainer buckets and cauldrons-was reaching not only Denmark, but Norway and Sweden also, and the weight system used during the Iron Age in Norway was based upon the Roman *denarius*.[149] This symbolized the economic influence of Rome across the region. Despite the economic blessings, the destruction of Rome/Babylon was the reaction of economic exploitation. The wealthy elite enjoy their luxurious life by oppressing the poor and the marginalized, peasants and farmers were the victims of this unjust economic structure. In following this, Bauckham opines that John sees a connection between Rome's economic affluence, Rome's idolatrous self-deification, and Rome's military and political brutality.[150] God's Judgement of Rome is also attributed to her slaughter of the innocent in general (18:24; cf. 18:6), her idolatrous arrogance (18:8), and her self-indulgence luxury at the expense of her empire (18:7). Therefore, John's attack on Rome in Revelation is aimed at the concrete political and economic realities

148 Howard-Brook, *Unveiling Empire*...171.

149 M. P. Charlesworth, *The Roman Empire* (Reprinted; London: Oxford University Press, 1961), 131.

150 Bauckham, *The Climax of Prophecy*, 349-50.

of the empire.[151] Indeed, the list of the cargoes is the evidence of the conspicuous wealth and extravagance of the rich families of Rome.

### *Pax Romana: A Hidden Slogan for Economic Exploitation*

In the period of Revelation, Rome offers for those who associate with her the supposed benefits of the *Pax Romana* which was launched in the Roman propaganda of this period. The *Pax Romana or Roman Peace* refers to a period in Roman history beginning with the reign of Augustus (27 B.C.E.) and ending with the death of Marcus Aurelius (180 C.E.). This was the era of relative calm and stability within the empire after long years of civil war and the threat of invasion. During this period, attention was given to peacetime activities, such as improving roads, increasing the food supply, and building adequate, temples, public baths and theatres. To keep the peace, the Romans tolerated various religious practices, as long as proper honour also was accorded to the emperor and to public rituals of Roman religions, resulting in the ongoing conflict for monotheistic Jews.[152] Rome offers the Mediterranean world unity, security, stability, and the conditions of prosperity. But, in John's view, these benefits are not what they seem: they are the favours of a prostitute, purchased at a high price. The *Pax Romana* is really a system of economic exploitation of the empire. Rome's subjects give far more to her than she gives to them. There are those who have vested interest in the power and the economic dominance of Rome: the kings, the merchants and the Mariners (18:9-19).[153] Many of

---

151 Bauckham, *The Climax of Prophecy,* 349-50.

152 (Marainne Blickenstaf, "Pax Romana," *NIDB*:421-422).

153 Bauckham, *The Climax of Prophecy,* 347. Harry O. Maier also argues Rev 17 recasts in the harlot the rhetorically named Jezebel of Rev 2:20, whose colourful Hebrew Bible career includes the charge of harlotry. Elisabeth Schüssler Fiorenza also views from rhetorical assessment and asserts that the image of the whore in Rev 17-18 does not speak about a female person or refer to actual historical wo/men, rather, Revelation deploys it as a figure of speech in order to characterise the idolatrous imperial power of Rome. It clearly depicts the connection between the image of the harlot and unjust socio-political and religious means. (See Harry O. Maier, "Staging the Gaze: Early Christian Apocalypses and Narrative Self-Representation," *in HTR* 90 (1997): 149-50; Elisabeth Schussler Fiorenza, "Babylon the Great: A Rhetorical Political

Rome's subjects are in fact exploited by her, yet fail to see it. They are dazzled by Rome's glory and seduced by the promised benefits of the *Pax Romana* and they fell into the trap of Pax Romana which becomes a hidden slogan for the economic exploitation.

## *Roman Slave Trade: A Symbol of Roman Economic Exploitation*

Rev 18:13b, the last list of trade goods of Rome ended by referencing "slaves ...and human lives" (NRSV). In ancient Rome slaves were commonly labelled "bodies," this underlies the status of the slave class.[154] They were not considered human beings but commodities that could be bought and sold. Revelation counters this way of looking at slaves by adding that the merchants were selling not only "bodies" but "the souls of human beings" (ψυχὰι ἀνθρώπων) Rev 18:13.[155] He further states that Slave trade was a hallmark of Roman commerce in Asia Minor, and it was an integral part of the local economies in the cities where John's readers lived. Inscriptions show that the network supplying the human cargo to meet the empire's demand extended into the marketplaces of Ephesus, Thyatira, and Sardis. Selling human bodies and souls was not a remote form of commerce but a familiar practice in the places where the readers lived (18:13). The slave dealers claimed a public place in society, but from the perspective of apocalypse, this simply brings the seamy underside of commerce with Rome into plain view.[156] M. I. Finley also asserts that a slave is a property, subject to the rules and procedures of property, with respect to the sale, lease, theft, natural

---

Reading of Revelation 17-18" in *The Reality of Apocalypse: Rhetoric and Politics in the Book of Revelation* Edited by David L. Barr. Atlanta: Society of Biblical Literature, 2006. 258).

154 Howard-Brook, *Unveiling Empire*..., 173. Slaves, in so far as they were objects of commerce, may be reckoned as luxury articles, for they were expensive and they were in the main purchased as personal servants. Slaves were used on a considerable scale in some areas for agriculture, but such slaves were almost always home born. (See A. H. M. Jones, *The Later Roman Empire 282-602* Vol. 2. UK: Basil Blackwell, 1986, 851).

155 Craig Koester, "Roman Slave Trade and the Critique of Babylon in Revelation 18" in *CBQ* (4 Oct 2008), 766-786.

156 Koester, "Roman Slave Trade and the Critique of Babylon in Revelation 18," 766-786.

increase and so on.[157] The Roman Economy was depended on the slave market, and, there is no doubt that the Slave-trade is one of the biggest markets in the Roman Empire, and she is the biggest slave trader in her contemporary.[158]

Slavery is an institution and the Roman Economy were primarily set up to benefit the city of Rome itself, one could say that the Roman Empire as it would have been impossible without slavery.[159] Slavery helped create the 1-2 percent leisure class of rulers, patricians, and others in Rome exempt from having to do any manual labour. Thus, when Rome falls or destroyed, this meant the end of the whole way of life for merchants and ship owners and those who depend on the wealth of Rome and slaves, on the other hand, to provide, transport, and deliver their goods.[160] Rome counts as a slave society in terms of the structural location of slavery: dominant groups relied to a significant degree of slave labour to generate a surplus and maintain their position of dominance.[161] The role of slavery in

157 C. I. David Joy, *Mark and Its Subalterns* (London: Equinox, 2008), 76. Warren Carter also opines that the Roman Economy was a slave-based economy. Slaves could be war captives, those born into slavery, abandoned children, those seized and sold by brigands, and, notably, adults enslaved as a result of debt. Slave conditions varied enormously depending on several factors, including the master, their skills, gender, attractiveness, and the physical strength of the slave. There is evidence of the brutal treatment of slaves (including unlimited sexual access) as well as genuine care. (See Warren Carter, "Economic Justice and the Roman Empire." Cited 11 July 2017. Online: http://www.bibleodyssey.org/en/passages/related-articles/economic-justice-and-the-roman-empire).

158 Aune, *Revelation 17-22 WBC Vol. 52C* (Texas: Word Books Publishers, 1997), 1002-3. The number of slaves in the Roman empire in the first century C.E. has been estimated at around ten million (i.e. 16.6-20% of the population), the majority of whom were male. According to Josephus, 97,000 Jewish prisoners were enslaved following in the first Jewish revolt of 66-73 C.E. Asia Minor, with the exception of the Roman province of Asia, was one of the regions most heavily exploited for slaves. Large scale slave trade took place regularly in the major cities of the Roman Empire, with Rome as the greatest of all slave markets

159 Witherington III, *Revelation,* 229-30.

160 Witherington III, *Revelation*, 230.

161 Walter Schneidel, *Slavery in the Roman Economy* (Standford: Standford University, 2010), 2.

central productive processes turned Rome into a 'slave economy' just as the widespread domination of slaves as a primary social relationship made it a 'slave society.'[162] In the Institute of the Roman jurist Gaius (130-180 C.E.) the slave is considered as commodities, that can be brought, owned, and sold at the will of the owner, slaves are denied the right to inherit property.[163] Thus, in Roman society, the slave trade is an institution which has its essential goal to carry out his task to the profit of his master.[164] Schneidel further describes that the Slaves were engaged in an enormous variety of activities, as estate managers, field hands, shepherds, hunters, domestic servants, craftsmen, construction workers, retailers, miners, clerks, teachers, doctor, midwives, wet-nurse, textile workers, potters, and entertainers. In addition to private sector employment, they worked in public administration and served in military support functions. Their responsibilities ranged from the most basic tasks of footmen and water-carriers to the complex duties of steward and business managers.[165]

The Romans learned how to make money through the slave trade, slavery thus provided the greatest amount of immediate income from the property.[166] In such an economic context, they have turned all the slaves into free day labourers to create an economy in which those at the bottom would have suffered even more insecurity and potential poverty than before.[167] The vast slave trade market was controlled by the ruling elite groups of Rome as they became the most profitable ones through the slave trade. This culture makes Rome as a slave society.

---

162 Schneidel, *Slavery in the Roman Economy*, 2.

163 Alejandro F. Botta, "Slaves, Slavery," *EDEJ*: 1232-1233.

164 Ceslas Spicq, *Theological Lexicon of the New Testament* Vol. 1. Translated by James D. Ernst (Masachusetts: Hendrickson, 1994), 383-384.

165 Schneidel, *Slavery in the Roman Economy*, 3.

166 S. S. Bartchy, "Slavery," *ISBE*: 539-546.

167 Bartchy, "Slavery," *ISBE*: 539-546.

## *Taxation in the Roman Empire: A Burden for Peasants and Common People*

Taxation was the main economic source of the Roman Empire. Taxation was extremely important for the emperor, and tax-powered enabled him, in some sense, to ensure his power/authority. It is not an exaggeration to say that census was an exercise of the Roman power and that taxation was rooted in the census.[168] While the ruling elite enjoys their lives, the peasants, farmers and the poor are always fighting for their survival. T. E. Schmidt said that there are three principal kinds of taxes in the Roman Empire: the land tax, the head tax (a periodic census Lk 2:1-5; Acts 5:37) and the customs (tolls and duties collected at ports and tax office near city gates).[169] As Hans-Josef Klauck asserts that the rulers take tax from their agricultural product, they took 30-70% taxes,[170] because of this, the people were very poor and difficult to survive because of the high taxes paid.

According to Menachem Elon (who had a fine study of Jewish taxation over the entire period of Jewish history), Tax is a compulsory payment, in currency or in species, exacted by a public authority, for the purpose of satisfying the latter's own needs or those of the public, or part of the public.[171] All the market, commercial and taxation

168 Pyung Soo Sea, *Luke's Jesus in the Roman Empire and the Emperor in the Gospel of Luke* (Eugene: Pickwick Publications, 2015), 55. Taxes paid during Roman Imperialism were: Soil tax, Market taxes, Transit tolls, Port taxes, Access rents, Head tax Denarius per year, labour for state projects. The taxation in Roman Palestine simply crushed the people as 50% of the fruits and 33% of the grains were taken as tax. The much-debated *Pax Romana* was maintained by the cruel and aggressive tax system. Roman colonial control, during the *Pax Romana* period, meant taxes, tolls, and levies of goods and labour (quoted by Joy, *Mark and Its Subalterns*, 76-77).

169 T. E. Schmidt, "Taxation, Jewish" in *DNTB*: 1163-1166.

170 Hans-Josef Klauck, "The Roman Empire," in Margaret M. Mitchell and Frances M. Young eds., *Origin to Constantine* (Cambridge: Cambridge University Press, 2006), 74.

171 As quoted in Robert A. Oden Jr., "Taxation in Biblical Israel" *JRE*, Vol. 12, No. 2 (Fall, 1984), 162-181, 163. The Roman economy was aggressive and centralized. Taxation was the basis for the relationship between landlords and peasants and the peasants gradually became landless tenants as they could not afford the burden of the imperial taxes. (See Joy, *Mark and Its Subalterns*, 76).

systems were controlled by the Romans under the supervision of the ruling elites. Hanson and Oakman observe that taxation in Roman Palestine was extractive, that is designed to assert the elite's control over agrarian taxes as Ceaser's agents collected taxes and redistributed them to the clients.[172] Rousseau and Arav's analysis of taxation would be helpful for a better understanding of the oppressed in Judea; they divided Roman taxation into three categories as Taxation by the Romans and Tetrarchs, Traditional Jewish Taxes, Forced exactions.[173]

Seo further mentioned the taxes given by the citizens of Rome as:

### *Taxation by the Roman and Tetrarchs*

1. *Tributum soli* on crops. Yearly average, excluding the sabbatical year: (25%+5x33%)/6 = 31.7%
   Estimated at 60% of all crops and income = 19%
2. *Tributum capitis*, for a family of six: 6 *denarii* of income for 250 days (one worker assumed) = 19%
3. Sales, inheritance taxes. Total impact = 5%
4. *Portorium*. Total impact = 4%
5. Gifts to official = 3%.
   Total civic taxes = 32%
   *Traditional Jewish Taxes*
   1. Tithes on all crops. Total impact = 8%
   2. Half-shekel (2 *dinarii*) tax on males = 1%
   3. Sacrifices. Toral impact = 3%
      Total Jewish Taxes = 12%

### *Forced Exactions*

1. Officials' persecution, banditry = 5%
   Total burden = 49%

172 Joy, *Mark and Its Subalterns*, 76.

173 Seo, *Luke's Jesus in the Roman Empire and the Emperor in the Gospel of Luke*, 66-67.

Besides, the taxes collected during the Roman reign included Soil tax, Market taxes, Transit tolls, Port taxes, Access rents, Head tax Denarius per year, Labour for state projects.[174]

In addition, the Temple taxation was another tax to be paid by the Jews which also become a burden for their lives. There are twelve main religious obligations for Jews, with tremendous financial implications in the life of the people as remarks by David Joy.[175]

The twelve main religious collections are as follows:

1. The sin offering.
2. Bickurim-the first fruit of the grain, grapes, figs and so on.
3. Terumah - 2% of the harvest.
4. The Tithe
5. Qallah-one twenty-fourth of the bread dough.
6. The first-born of animals.
7. Redemption money for the firstborn child = 5 shekel = two weeks' wages for labourers in Palestine.
8. Parts of animals slaughtered for food and part of the wool at sheep-shearing.
9. Extraordinary dues.
10. The annual ½ shekel tax.
11. The annual wood-gathering for the Temple.
12. Free-will offering to the Temple.

In fact, these taxes become a burden for the citizen. People should work hard for their survival despite a heavy tax paid. The tax problems arise in the whole inhabited empire, due to the excessive demands of the tax collector, peasants would not have participated in the market economy.

Tax and tributes, usually collected in kind, transferred wealth from peasant farmers, fishermen, local artisans and workers to local landowners, regional officials, and the emperor. Detailed information on taxes in most part of the empire is scarce.[176] Refusal to pay taxes

174 Joy, *Mark and Its Subalterns,* 76.

175 Joy, *Mark and Its Subalterns,* 109.

176 Warren Carter, *John and Empire: Initial Explorations* (New York: T&T Clark, 2008), 56.

was considered as an act of rebellion.[177] Taxation is one of the main sources of Rome. The expansion of the empire benefited many Roman businessmen; military conquest opened up new areas for real estate speculation, trade, banking, and government contracts. Among the most lucrative government contracts were those dealing with the collection of public revenues. These public revenues include not only harbour taxes and customs tariffs but, more importantly, indemnities and poll taxes.[178] Apart from this, the Roman government take taxes from the religious sites and various forms of taxes from the citizens too. These corporations made a profit and are the main beneficiaries of the Roman Empire.

Because of the tax problem, the pride of Rome-*Pax Romana* was criticised and found that it was the manifesto of Roman political propaganda since it was maintained by the cruel and aggressive tax system. Carter criticizes that taxes were a standard way of imposing the imperial will.[179] In relation to this tax system, many necessary menial jobs were performed cheaply by the slaves and the cost of administration was very low. Even the tax system was heavy and a burden for the people. Under Roman rule, many small landowners

---

177 Stephen Dyson, "Native Revolts in the Roman Empire." *Historia 20* (1971), 239-74.

178 Jo-Ann Shelton, *As the Romans Did: A Source Book in Roman Social History* (New York: Oxford University Press, 1998), 143. An indemnity was a large sum of money paid by a conquered nation to Rome in order to compensate Rome for the expenses it occurred in fighting the war. A poll tax was an annual tax paid to Rome to reimburse it for the cost of maintaining a governor and a military force in a province.

179 Warren Carter, "Paying the Tax to Rome as Subversive Praxis: Matthew 17.24-27" *JSNT76* (1999): *3-31*. Therefore, tax problems become serious critical issues in the Roman Empire. Friedrich, Pohlmann, and Stuhlmacher argued that the tax protests of 58 C.E. and the eviction of the Jews from Rome in 49 meant that Paul was keen that returning Jewish residents of Rome, such as Prisca and Aquila, did not draw attention to themselves by not paying their taxes. Strobel also argued that in the time of Claudius there was widespread dissatisfaction over the granting to procurators of the right to levy taxes. It was Nero who increases the level of taxes toward the end of his reign, introducing a new tax on tenants' payable retrospectively for twelve months to the Privy Purse. (See Oakes, *Rome in the Bible and the Early Church*, 84-5).

lost their lands due to the aggressive and oppressive tax system.[180] This research proved that taxation becomes a burden for the common citizen of Rome. In addition, the taxation system of Romans became the economic exploitation upon the ordinary people, peasants, marginalised and the subalterns.

## 3.8. Conclusion

This chapter helps us to understand the situation of the background and also the milieu of socio-political and economic scenario of the Roman Empire including the Christian communities in the early centuries. Even though scholars are debating the identity of Babylon, but as it has been mentioned earlier, after a profound study done by scholars it is appropriate to conclude that the symbolism of Babylon in Revelation is none other than Rome and its empire. This research follows Rome as Babylon and would further precede accordingly the usage of Babylon as Rome. The study of economic issues in Rev 18 portrays the economic crime committed by Rome. This survey clearly shows the scenario of the Roman economic condition and also the unjust economic system in the empire.

180 Joy, *Mark and Its Subalterns,* 78.

Chapter 4

# Final Judgment Upon the Unjust Economic Wealth of Rome A Socio-Rhetorical Reading of Revelation 18

## 4.1. Introduction

The socio-rhetorical reading of Revelation 18 along with the postcolonial lens[181] was employed in this chapter by doing the exegetical study of the text. Following Vernon, this approach gives special attention to the subjects and topics a text uses to present thought, speech, stories, and arguments, it integrates the ways people use language with the ways they live in the world.[182] This rhetorical

181 Postcolonial theory is an attempt to 'interrupt' to read 'contrapuntally' and 'interrogatively' the tragic experiences of those dispossessed of voice and discriminated against, those 'who have suffered the sentence of history,' in order, instead, to formulate critical revisions of cultural differences and 'empowering strategies of emancipations.' (Homi Bhabha, *The Location of Culture* London: Routledge, 2004, 246).

182 Robbins, *Exploring the Texture of Texts: A Guide to Socio-Rhetorical Interpretation*, 1. Socio-Rhetorical Criticism was emerged in the 1970s and received its name in 1984 with the integration of rhetorical, anthropological and social-psychological insights in a study of the Gospel of Mark. Socio-rhetorical interpretation began with analysis and interpretation of social and

study gives attention to the subjects and topics by which reason this tool was inserted in doing exegesis in this chapter. The exegetical study was divided into five main sections according to the biblical verses concluded with the final judgment of God upon Rome; each section reflects the economic injustice of Rome and portrays the real identity of Roman capitalism.

## 4.2. Introduction to Revelation 18

Revelation 18 draws on a repertoire of biblical laments and anti-imperial strategies to portray Rome as doomed and to appeal to readers to "come out" of the city's unjust economy. It is a complex of images and prophetic proclamations, tightly modelled on biblical traditions.[183] As Nelson Kraybill observes, these passages of the great prophets' deal with the interplay of Empire, commerce, and idolatry; they help explain author's attitude toward Rome and his reasons for rejecting economic involvement with her.[184] While chapter (17) focuses on the critique of Rome's politics, Rev 18 focuses on the

---

cultural dynamics in written works. It is an approach to literature that focuses on values, convictions, and beliefs both in the texts we read and in the world in which we live, this approach leads to the detailed attention to the text itself, it moves interactively into the world of the people who wrote the texts and into our present world. He further states that it evaluates and reorients its strategies and it engages in multi-faceted dialogue with the texts and other phenomena that comes within its purview, which means that it invites methods and methodological results into the environment of its activities. David deSilva also asserts that Rhetorical analysis offers a wealth of insights into the way in which an NT text sought to persuade its hearers to take a particular course of action. Thus, the goal of socio-rhetorical interpretation is to bring skills we use on a daily basis into an environment of interpretation that is both intricately sensitive to detail and perceptive attentive to large fields of meanings in the world in which we live. (See Vernon K. Robbins, "Socio-Rhetorical Interpretation" in *The Blackwell Companion to the New Testament.* Edited by David Aune. London: Wiley Blackwell, 2010, 192; David A. DeSilva, *Perseverance in Gratitude: A Socio-Rhetorical Commentary on the Epistle to the Hebrews.* Grand Rapids: Eerdmans, 2000), 39; Robbins, *Exploring the Texture of Texts: A Guide to Socio-Rhetorical Interpretation*, 2).

183 Rossing, *The Choice Between Two Cities*, 99.

184 J. Nelson Kraybill, *Imperial Cult and Commerce in John's Apocalypse*, *JSNT* Sup 132 (Sheffield: Sheffield Academic Press, 1996), 161.

critique of Rome's economy. Economic critique takes centre stage in Rev 18 with indictments of the merchants at the opening and close of the chapter, and adaptation of Ezekiel's oracles against Tyre's maritime trade at its centre.[185] Thus, the whole chapter depicts the economic issue of Rome and her final judgment of God.

## 4.3. The Fall of Babylon (Rome): 18:1-3

### *Introduction*

This verse portrays the most memorable and negative pictures of Rome in extant literature and is crafted to foreground the multiple levels of injustice that inhere in Roman imperialism, depicting the Roman domination system and indignation at its practices, propaganda, and successes.[186] The pronouncement of the fall of Babylon-Rome[187] in Revelation is one of the most negative pictures of Rome in NT. The angel has great authority (different from other angels) from above announces the destruction of Rome. This destruction affects not only of Rome but also her inhabitants and partners.

### *Exegetical Notes*

The destruction of Babylon has been predicted. It (destruction of Babylon) bears a great resemblance to Jeremiah's depiction of doom on ancient Babylon (Jer 50:39; 51:37). The sign of the total destruction of the city (in Jeremiah) is that wild animals now live in the ruins. It is no longer fit for human habitation. In Rev 18:2, Babylon has become the home of hateful birds and beasts.[188] The city of Rome (Babylon) in Revelation was such a mighty and powerful

---

185 Rossing, *The Choice Between Two Cities,* 100.

186 David A. deSilva, *Seeing things John's Way: The Rhetoric of the Book of Revelation* (Louisville: John Knox Press, 2009), 203.

187 Some scholar (Moffat) assume that some sort of Jewish sources lies behind this section that breathed the indignant spirit of a Jewish apocalyptic against the proud empire which had won a temporary triumph over the city and people of God and was taken over by John for the purpose of making Rome responsible for the persecution of Christians (Robert H. Mounce, *The Book of Revelation NICNT* (Revised Edition; Grand Rapids: Eerdmans, 1998), 322).

188 Gonzalez, *Revelation,* 116.

city. It did control the economic life of vast areas and therefore could survive. As its height, about John's time, it had a population of about one million. By the sixth century, after the defeat of its armies, the loss of its economic base, and the effects of invasion, famine, and disease, the city of Rome had only about 30,000 inhabitants. In such a situation, it would not be at all surprising to find that wild animal had come well within the old city limits, now abandoned by human beings.[189] The angel (who announced the destruction) has a 'great authority' and it does not question from where did the angel got that authority. Μετὰ ταῦτα indicates what comes next in the sequence of visions John received, this phrase generally introduces something new, denoting a new commencement and a new set of circumstances.[190] The angel has ἐξουσί αν μεγάλην (great authority) which some have related to his role as executor of the judgment he is to announce,[191] this phrase occurs only in Revelation in the NT although Greek πασα ἐξουσί αν 'all authority' is found quite frequently.[192] καταβαίνοντα ἐκ τοῦ οὐρανοῦ also signifies the authority that comes from the above which cannot be judged from the earth and is superior to the earth.

David deSilva assumed that the mighty angel as Christ who holds the supreme authority, in such a manner, here John proclaims God as the *Pantokratōr* (cf. 15:3 παντοκράτωρ), the one who holds all things within his grasp. This God consistently appears as one sitting enthroned, a posture declaring that God reigns over the cosmos.[193] The noun παντοκράτωρ appears 9 times in Revelation, the interpretation of the epithet as "Yahweh the powerful" or "Yahweh the almighty" correspond to the primary translation found in the LXX, κυριος παντοκράτωρ, the primary

189 Gonzalez, *Revelation,* 116.

190 Robert L. Thomas, *Revelation 8-22 an Exegetical Commentary* (Chicago: Moody Publishers, 1995), 314.

191 Thomas, *Revelation 8-22,* 314.

192 J. Massyngberde Ford, *Revelation-The Anchor Bible* (New York: Doubleday, 1975), 296.

193 deSilva, *Seeing things John's Way,* 165.

sense is "almighty."[194] God the Almighty, θεὸς ὁ παντοκράτωρ (cf. Rev 15:3 BNT) signifies God's justice in the unrighteous;[195] it also intends to make visible the omnipotence and absolute reign of God.[196] The appearance of the descending angel may be a Christophany comparable to appearances of "the angel of the LORD" in the OT (cf. 10:1; Eze 43:2), the angels strong voice highlighting the authority of the announcement of Babylon's fall, the authoritative nature of announcement is stressed here.[197] John observes that this angel 'exercised great authority,' which points to the divine origin and therefore the importance of the message to be delivered.[198]

The angel's proclamation Επεσεν ἔπεσεν Βαβυλὼν ἡ μεγάλη (Fallen, fallen is Babylon the great!) is a deliberate echo of 14:8; and the repetition ties together the seventh sign of angelic judgment in scene 4 with the announcement of impending destruction here.[199] This phrase has also the OT background to this threnody in Isa 21:9 (Fallen, fallen is Babylon; and all the images of her gods lie shattered on the ground). The whore-like city will become a dwelling for demons, evil spirits, and unclean and detestable birds and beast. Elsewhere in the apocalypse, the demonic realm is associated with idolatry (cf. 2:20, 24; 9:20); so that the demons and evil spirits of this verse become a symbol for Babylon's devilish nature, masked until now behind a deceitful disposition towards idolatry.[200]

The word τῆς γῆς (of the earth v. 3) denotes the mass of mankind as it does so often in this book. The merchants will suffer more than the kings because the kings will have their political power left. Commerce and trade are the major subjects of the remainder

---

194 H. Langkammer, "παντοκράτωρ" *EDNT*: 11-12. He further states that Rev 1:8 is a divine saying. It is asyndetically joined to the preceding clause, which is intended to demonstrate that the end of the world is in God's hands (v. 7).

195 Beale, *The Book of Revelation,* 795.

196 Langkammer, "παντοκράτωρ" *EDNT*: 11-12.

197 Beale, *The Book of Revelation*, 892-3.

198 Smalley, *The Revelation to John,* 443.

199 Smalley, *The Revelation to John,* 443.

200 Smalley, *The Revelation to John*, 444.

of the chapter.[201] The word πορνει, (v. 3) means immorality, unlawful sexual acts; the figure is also used for apostasy and idolatry (cf. Rev 17:1).[202]

The three groups of people (mourners) mentioned in verse 3 portray the identity of the colleague of Rome. The *first group*, all nations who are drunk, πέπωκαν (have drunk), apparently, the οινος[203] (wine) they drink was deliberately sinning against God, and it cannot be forgiven.[204] Τηε σεχονδ γρουπ, βασιλεῖς τῆς γῆς is the kings who joined Rome and shared her wealth at the expense of their own integrity.[205] They loved luxury as she did, they commit spiritual adultery with Babylon (17:2), and that is, they give leadership by pursuing religious, political, and economic goals. They worship idols, rule harshly, and enrich themselves at the expense of others who are less fortunate than them. Since money is their idol, they force all their subordinates to pay homage to this god.[206] The *third group* is ἔμποροι (merchant) of the world. In the time of Revelation, Rome was the storehouse of all the products and produce in the ancient world.[207] It can be possibly comparable with today's Multinational Corporations dominate the world trade. As a consequence, the rich increase their assets and display their opulence while the indigent

---

201 Thomas, *Revelation 8-22,* 318-19.

202 Fritz Rienecker, *A Linguistic Key to the Greek New Testament* (Grand Rapids: Zondervan Publishing House, 1980), 851.

203 Revelation used oinoς to portray the punishment that God gives to the godless to drink like wine (the wine of God's wrath 14:10; 16:19; 19:15) and in speaking of "the wine (of the wrath) of the adultery" of Babylon. (Horst Balz and Gerhard Schneider, *EDNT*, Volume 2. (Reprinted; Grand Rapids: Eerdmans, 2000), 505.

204 Simon J. Kistemaker, *New Testament Commentary-Exposition of the Book of Revelation* (Grand Rapids: Baker Books, 2001), 487.

205 Clifton J. Allen ed., *Revelation-BBC Vol-12* (USA: Broadman Press, 1972), 336.

206 Kistemaker, *New Testament Commentary,* 487.

207 Kistemaker, *New Testament Commentary,* 487. The word for merchants, *ἔμποροι* comes from combining *ἐν* (in) and *πορος* (journey), a merchant is one of the journeys to conduct business. In ancient times, the merchants of Tyre were renowned throughout the world (Isa. 23:8).

copes with poverty.[208] As a result, the distance between the rich and the poor became more comprehensive and worse.

### *Comments*

The above exegesis proved the subject of the passage in large part is materialism and greed-the wrongful orientation toward good things of this world. As David Joy remarks that Rome was representing the culmination of all evil structures and forces including luxurious life,[209] it is very important to see the connection between the economic power of a city, especially a city that is the capital of an empire, and the ease with which the city can be destroyed when its economic power is gone.[210] Revelation focuses on the attack of not Babylon's physical or architectural structure, but on its trade and commerce and her alliances. The assurance of Babylon's destruction from the superior authority through the angel remarks the seriousness of economic sins committed against God.

## 4.4. Abstain from Economic Sin: "Come out of my People": 18:4-8

### *Introduction*

In Rev 18, the primary vehicle for Babylon's destruction is not a "holy war" but a legal trial in which a "class action suit" is brought on behalf of Babylon's victim.[211] Rev 17 introduced the Babylon vision as "judgment" (κριαις), this central focus on judgment continues in Rev 18 with multiple references to judgment.[212] In this passage, the people of God[213] (who are not involved in the luxurious sins of Rome) are called out to set apart themselves from Rome so that they may not share their sins and escape from the divine judgment of

208 Kistemaker, *New Testament Commentary*, 487.

209 Joy, *Revelation-A Post-colonial View Point*, 77.

210 Gonzalez, *Revelation*, 116.

211 Elisabeth Schussler Fiorenza, *The Book of Revelation: Justice and Judgement* (Philadelphia: Fortress Press, 1985), 7.

212 Rossing, *The Choice Between Two Cities*, 118.

213 Scholars like Clifton J. Allen opines that 'the people' here refers to the 'early Christians.'

Rome. In the previous verse, the author focuses only on the Babylon-Rome, but here, it focuses on the faithful people of God, to abstain them from the sins of economic Rome. In other words, it can be called a call of God's people to separate them from the materialistic unjust economy of Babylon.

## *Exegetical Notes*

The author here shifts the dimension/image of Babylon from rather than attacking the battlefield (which is typical for city laments and siege narratives) to a courtroom. In shifting this, the author draws an element of Jeremiah 50-51 and other military oracles but transfer them to fit a legal context. Schussler Fiorenza demonstrates that in the overall rhetoric of the book the author deliberately subordinates divine warfare language to judicial language and prophetic judgment.[214] The shift from military siege to courtroom lawsuit strategy against Babylon is evident in Revelation's use of and transformation of Jeremiah's anti-Babylon imperative commands. The command of Jer 51:45 "My people, come out from her, and let everyone save himself from the fierce anger of the LORD" (NRSV) issues several strings of military imperatives calling on an unnamed audience to "raise shouts," "take up positions," "shoot," "come against her," "kill," "sharpen arrows," "prepare ambushes" and engaged in other military activities to "prepare the nations for war against her.[215] The imperatives of Rev 18:4-7 are crucial to the rhetorical reading of Revelation in order to understand the divine judgment of Rome.

*Come out of Babylon-* Εξέλθατε ὁ λαός μου ἐξ αὐτῆς (18:4), The call to come out of Babylon in Rev 18:4 is the rhetorical key to the entire Babylon vision. Readers must come out of Babylon in order to enter into Gods' New Jerusalem.[216] The aorist imperative form of 'Εξέλθατε (come out) in verse 4 expresses the urgency of the call. The vocative ὁ λαός with the personal pronoun μου indicates that the first part of this statement (vv 4-5) addresses the faithful,

214 Fiorenza, *The Book of Revelation: Justice and Judgement*, 169.

215 David J. Reimer, *The Oracles against Babylon in Jeremiah 50-51: A Horror among the Nations* (San Francisco: Mellen Research University Press, 1993), 161.

216 Rossing, *The Choice Between Two Cities,* 120.

they are primarily those alive at the apex of the beast's kingdom and yet-to-come climax of the Babylonian system.[217] Collins argues that whether the command is to be read literally or metaphorically as an appeal to the audience to withdraw from economic interaction with Babylon,[218] to cease participation in the imperial cult.[219] The purpose of separating is not only 'not to partake of her sins,' but to escape the coming judgment, and it does not mean that Christians are not being called to withdraw from economic life, nevertheless, they may be ostracized from the sphere of economic dealings because of their refusal to compromised with unjust economic system.[220]

The call of Rev 18:4 to "come out" is followed by four more second plural imperatives in Rev 18:6-7, calling on an unnamed audience to take four actions:[221]

4.3.2.1. to give back (ἀπόδοτε) to Babylon as it gave to others;

4.3.2.2. to "double" (διπλώσατε) according to Babylon's own works,

4.3.2.3. to "mix" (κεράσατε) a double strength potion in Babylon's own cup;

4.4.2.4. to "give" (δότε) Babylon a proportional dose of its own torture and grief.

Likewise in the imperatives of Rev 18:4 and 18:20, these four commands are followed by ὅτι clauses that signify the reason for these imperatives. As several rhetorical theorists mark the importance of the audience witnessing the speaker's own genuine experience of emotions as a catalyst for the stirring of their own,[222] here, John emphasizes the anger of God by mentioning the divine judgment upon Babylon.

---

217 Thomas, *Revelation 8-22,* 321.

218 J. J. Collins, "The Political Perspective of the Revelation to John" *JBL* 96/2 (1977), 241-256.

219 Kraybill, *Imperial Cult and Commerce in John's Apocalypse*, 161.

220 Beale, *The Book of Revelation,* 898.

221 Rossing, *The Choice Between Two Cities,* 122.

222 deSilva, *Seeing things John's Way*, 209.

The audience for the four imperatives of Rev 18:6-7 is a key interpretive question in Revelation 18. Who is being called to give back, double, and mix this cup of Babylon? Since the grammatical tense, voice, person, and a number of these imperatives is the same as that of the previous imperative to "come out" in Rev 18:4,[223] scholars solved the problem of the audience of Rev 18:6-7 by invoking various unnamed groups to carry out the retributive imperatives. Swete argues the audience as of course not to the 'people of God,' but to the ministers of Divine justice, the yet untrained and unknown forces which the Seer (author) saw gathering for the work of destruction.[224] The legal proportionality of the imperatives of Rev 18:6-7 is emphasized by repeated correlatives 'just a' (ὡς, Rev 18:6; ὅσα, Rev 18:7) and the note that Babylon's fate is 'in accordance with its deeds' (κατὰ τὰ ἔργα αὐτῆς). 'Double' (διπλοω, διπλώσατε Rev 18:6) is not an indiscriminate escalation of violence, but rather the legally prescribed repayment for one who has committed a crime.[225] The torment and grief that the audience is called to 'give' (δοτε) to Babylon are correlated proportionately to the glory that Babylon should have 'give' (δοτε, 14:7, 19:7) to God.

The political and economic arrogance noted in v 7b is emphasized as the cause (διὰ τοῦτο) for Babylon's sudden destruction. In the end, John assure his audience that the unchallenging status of divine sovereignty by mentioning Babylon was demolished by the OT concept of God's armour like plaque (πληγαι), famine (λιμός) within a single day, God's judgment is severing in strength, whereas Babylon, even if she has pretensions to rule as a queen.

### Comments

The above rhetorical reading of the passage clearly portrays that the arrogance of Rome-Babylon (in terms of economic capitalism) causes divine judgment. Bauckham also affirms that the primary meaning

223 Rossing, *The Choice Between Two Cities,* 122.

224 Swete, *The Apocalypse of St. John,* 229.

225 Kenneth Strand "Some Modalities of Symbolic Usage in Revelation 18" *AUSS* 24 (1986), 37-46.

of the harlot image in Rev 17-18 is economic.[226] In the OT, Babylon stands as a symbol of crime and destruction so also in NT Rome was pictured as a symbol of harlots, destruction, crime and also a powerful and influential. As David Joy mentioned that the sins of Rome referring to processor state of idolatry, misuse of power, sexual abuse and disorder, corruption and dehumanising activities of the people of God, and misled many nations into committing sin against God and the people of God. Trade (in terms of unjust economy) is placed as a major crime because the profit is made by exploiting the poor and the downtrodden of the community.[227] An important facet of Christian witness involves coming out from Babylon, disentangling oneself from violence and exploitative economics and from seeking and sharing in the benefits of unjust practices. God's commitment to justice-to vindicate the deaths of the innocent and the faithful ones, and to visit destruction upon those who have afflicted, or collaborated with those who inflict, destructive practices upon the earth and its inhabitants impels us to learn how to "come out from Babylon" both to witness to God's justice and to avoid falling afoul of God's justice.[228] By knowing this, the people of God are warned to abstain themselves from the sin of Rome so that they may be escaped from the divine judgment. The passage portrays the sovereignty of God and His judgment was beyond challenge.

## 4.5. The Mourners of Economic Rome: 18:9-19

### *Introduction*

Rev 18:9-19 portrays the fall of Babylon from the perspective of Babylon's collaborators-the kings, merchants, and mariners/ shipmasters and sailors who lament their great loss. This lament has a parallel to Ezekiel's satirical laments[229] against the maritime empire

---

226 Bauckham, *The Climax of Prophecy,* 348.

227 Joy, *Revelation*, 79.

228 deSilva, *Seeing Things John's Way*, 344.

229 The prophetic oracles against Tyre in Ezekiel 26-28 are the lengthiest condemnation of any foreign power in Ezekiel's oracles against foreign nations. Drawing on Tyre's location as a rocky island on the Phoenician coast. Ezekiel's metaphors of judgment revolve around the sea. Ezekiel challenges Tyre's

of Tyre (Eze 26-28). Ezekiel's laments (in OT) serve as the model for the central three-fold dirge section of Revelation 18. Since they are the economic partner of Rome, they mourned with the fall of Babylon, not because of the pity of the people inside but the loss of their trade and business which also signifies their selfishness by neglecting.

## *Exegetical Notes*

The passage clearly mentions that the collaborators who had depended on Rome break out into weeping and mourning, watching the smoke rise from the city at a distance, they are weeping over their own loss, they mourn only over their own economic demise and do not perceive even at this final point in history that their loss involves much more than loss of material security.[230] They think only of the implications for themselves, such as the fallen, selfish human nature.

The first group of mourners οἱ βασιλεῖς τῆς γῆς (v. 9 the kings of the earth) express the most impersonal of the laments and stand the farthest away from the destruction of Babylon,[231] the kings regret having lost their power so suddenly (18:10). The kings are careful to distance themselves from the grim sight as they witness Babylon's burning, they are fascinated by the horrifying blaze. The kings of the earth refer not just to the client kings who put their kingdoms

---

false sense of security as an impenetrable "rock of Gibaltrar" dominating the whole Eastern Mediterranean. In an ironic metaphorical turn, the very force from which Tyre draws its strength, the sea, becomes the instrument of its destruction. God throws Tyre down into the sea, so that "you will never be found again" (Eze 26:21; cf. Rev 18:21). Ezekiel 27 is the most commercial Ezekiel's Tyre oracles, and the oracle most important to Revelation. Ezekiel raises a "lamentation" (*qinah*) over Tyre, portraying the city as a great merchant ship constructed of wood and the world's finest luxury materials, and rowed by an international crew. The detailed prose listing of the ship's cargoes acquired from nations all over the world (Eze 27:12-24) gives a powerful sense of Tyre's wealth and commercial reach. The magnitude of the economic disaster is appalling. Ezekiel conveys the enormity of the devastation through the laments of two elite wealthy groups (powerful princes and seafarers) who are devastated by Tyre's fall. (See Rossing, *The Choice Between Two Cities,* 130-131).

230 Beale, *The Book of Revelation*, 906.

231 Aune, *Revelation 17-22 WBC,* 978.

under the umbrella of the Roman Empire, but more generally to the local ruling classes whom throughout the empire Rome co-opted to a share in her rule.[232] The power they shared with Rome's certainly had economic advantages, which also means they shared with Rome's luxury and they are the ruling classes who benefitted with Rome, and they became one of the main reasons of the gap between rich and poor widened.

When the oppressive economic system of Rome collapse, the second group of mourners ἔμποροι τῆς γῆς (v. 11 merchants of the earth), are also described as 'your (i.e., Babylon's) merchants'. This does not mean that they were Romans, but simply that they did business with the city of Rome. Most of the merchants engaged in the trade with Rome, even those residents in Puteoli, Ostia, and Rome, were provincials, citizens of the exporting cities from which the merchandise came.[233] In the early period, the merchants had their own standard weights. There was no National Bureau of Standards at that time. In quest of greater profits, the merchant frequently cut corners or cheated the buyer outright. Sometimes, with pride and self-exaltation they vaunted their increased wealth. Because of such a bearing, they came under God's condemnation. Revelation 18 picks up a similar motif in the lamentation against Babylon, the obstinate enemy of God. The merchant had grown wealthy from Babylon's extreme extravagance (v. 3). Now that she was gone, so was their source of wealth (v. 11). Thus, they became mourners at her departure, but they wept at a distance, fearing that her torment would become theirs (v. 15). Babylon's merchants were a significant means by which her false ideology and religion reached distant places and held peoples bound and consequently they participated fully in her judgment.[234] John refers accurately to their wealth, which put many of them among the richest men of their time, and to their

---

232 Bauckham, *The Climax of Prophecy*, 372. John's reader in the province of Asia Minor will have thought most obviously of the local aristocracy who sat on the councils of their cities. For such people, Roman authority served to prop up their own dominant position in society.

233 T. Frank ed., *An Economic Survey of Ancient Rome* Vol. 5 (Baltimore: John Hopkins Press, 1940), 242.

234 J. E. Hartley, "Merchant" *ISBE*: 322

considerable economic power, as banded together in the trading companies and associations.[235] The third group Καὶ πᾶς κυβερνήτης (v.17 sailors/shipmasters) are also described to include all who were employed in the maritime transport industry, they made themselves a living from the trade with Rome by sea.[236] It is seen that the three-fold laments of Rev 18:9-19 clearly communicate to the people (audience) that they will not be so fortunate unless they 'come out' of Babylon. Those who stay and allied with its evil economy and idolatrous empire of Rome/Babylon have no hope.

## *Comments*

The whole passage of lamentation allows us to see the fall of Rome from a very definite perspective which was certainly not John's: the perspective of those who depended for power and wealth or simply for a living on their involvement with Rome and her economic system.[237] John depicted the empire as a network of cynical, blasphemous, self-interested political alliances that will self-destruct according to God's will; this new accusation allowed John to lay out a sarcastic description of the interplay of imperialism, political collaboration and economic exploitation in the rest of Revelation 18.[238] So, for those people who depended on economic Rome and participate in the luxurious and excess economic unjust corruption of Rome, the fall of Rome was a great loss and also disaster for them too. Because their trade and business were damaged also their profit and interest were in vain. They mourn for their loss, not for the pity of the city and her people. This also signifies their corrupted mind and crime against God.

---

235 Bauckham, *The Climax of Prophecy*, 373.

236 Bauckham, *The Climax of Prophecy*, 374.

237 Bauckham, *The Climax of Prophecy*, 374.

238 Steven J. Friesen, "Satan's Throne, Imperial Cults and the Social Settings of Revelation" *JSNT* 27.3 (2005), 351-373.

## 4.6. The Wealth of Rome-List of Cargoes: 18:11-13

### *Introduction*

The Roman Empire in the early centuries was of great wealth than we imagine. This passage listed the cargoes that have been used for trade and commerce which portrays the global worldwide business of the Roman Empire. Here, John listed twenty-eight items of merchandise imported by sea to the city of Rome. From this list of cargoes, it can assume the wealth of Rome and the expansion of the trade system and business in a worldwide. The wealth of Rome was beyond measured and their economic status reached its peak.

### *Exegetical Notes*

The verse opened with the mourning of the merchants, Babylon is the epitome of luxury, so with her gone, and no one remained to buy their commodities. They had made money their god, using unscrupulous means to accumulate material goods and placing their whole confidence in this centre of commerce. Primarily they bemoan the loss of profits and customers, but they also grieve over the disappearance of so great a treasure as this city represents (v. 11).[239]

Verses 12-13 listed the articles in merchandise. The economic and commercialism of Babylon with its materialistic emphasis on consumerism is clearly seen in the list of cargoes. Commercial trade in ancient times was far-flung, also international and varied. Swete argues that merchandise came to Rome by sea direct from such ports as Seleucid, Ephesus, Smyrna, Corinth, Alexandria, Carthage, which tapped the resources of the East and of Africa, and on the West from Marseilles and Spain.[240] The merchant and the maritime traders are more grounded than the rulers in the historical situation of luxury and wealth which belonged to the Mediterranean world of the first century C.E.[241] A representative list of trade products shows what *cargo* will no longer be purchased by the Babylonian economic system. The items were applied to a personification of the

239 Thomas, *Revelation 8-22,* 331.

240 Swete, *The Apocalypse of St. John*, 232.

241 Smalley, *The Revelation to John*, 453.

Babylonian economic system in 17:4[242] and John mentions accurately to their wealth, which put many of them among the richest men of their time, and to their considerable economic power[243] and also as Rome needed thousands of collaborating merchants to maintain its standard of living.[244] The items of cargo featured in the corrupt trading systems of Rome, it is a representative collection, reflecting the economic attractiveness of a systematic evil seduces rulers and merchants into unfaithful and idolatrous relationships with the scarlet woman.[245]

The list of articles mentioned in vv. 12-13 can be categorised into seven: 1) Precious wares (gold, silver, stone, pearls); 2) Materials of rich attire (fine linen, silk, purple, scarlet); 3) Material for costly furniture (all kinds of scented wood, all articles of Ivory, all articles of costly woods, bronze, iron, and marble); 4) Precious spices (cinnamon, spice, incense, myrrh, frankincense); 5) Articles of food (wine, olive oil, choice flour and wheat); 6) Merchandised for agricultural and domestic uses (cattle, sheep, horses and chariots); 7) Traffic in men (slaves, human lives).

### *Precious Wares (gold, silver, pearls)*

#### *Gold (χρυσοῦ) and Silver* (ἀργύρου*), Jewels (*λίθου τιμίου*-precious stone) and Pearls* (μαργαριτῶν)

The first four items were grouped together because of their similarities. Rome imported gold especially from Spain, where most of the mines had become state property during the first century,[246] and it came from western Romania.[247] The use of gold was one of the commonly noticed features of the growth of extravagant luxury among the wealthy families of Rome in the first century.[248] Again,

242 Beale, *The Book of Revelation*, 909.

243 Bauckham, *The Climax of Prophecy*, 373.

244 J. Nelson Kraybill, *Apocalypse and Allegiance: Worship, Politics and Devotion in the Book of Revelation* (Grand Rapids: Brazos Press, 2010), 148.

245 Smalley, *The Revelation to John*, 453.

246 Bauckham, *The Climax of Prophecy*,352.

247 Kistemaker, *New Testament Commentary*, 494.

248 Bauckham, *The Climax of Prophecy*, 352.

this metal of gold adorned the homes of wealthy families in Rome and was used to make regal and religious objects.[249]

*Silver* (ἀργύρου) also originated in Spain and imported, and was used to embellished couches, cups, and plates. Pliny strongly associates silver with the luxury of the Roman rich in his time, remarking on the fashions for silver-plated couches and baths made silver, the common use of silver for serving food.[250] Like gold, silver typified luxury through its common use for silver-plate couches, baths made of silver, its customary use to make implements for serving food, and the like.[251] It again symbolizes the wealth of Rome.

*Precious Stones* (λίθου τιμίου) mostly come from India and were cut and polished in Alexandria,[252] Rome had the wealth to import them, and love for them to grow to a violent passion during the first century. Women wear them in large quantities and men had them set in rings for them to wear.[253]

*Pearls* (μαργαριτῶν), low-grade pearls came from the Red Sea and the highest quality from the Persian Gulf, but the largest numbers were from India. By the end of the first century, they may have constituted the majority of oriental trade. Citizens of Rome valued pearls below diamonds but were willing to pay more for very large, high-quality pearls. Pearls epitomized Rome's increasing turn to extravagant luxury.[254] Pliny said that pearls were the costliest product of the sea in those days.[255]

## *Material of Rich Attire (Fine Linen, Purple, Silk, Scarlet)*

*Fine Linen* (βυσσίνου): It refers to the garments made from the Egyptian flax.[256] In the first century, it was tending to replace wool as clothing in Rome. John here refers to the expensive linen worn by

249 Kistemaker, *New Testament Commentary,* 494.

250 Bauckham, *The Climax of Prophecy,* 352.

251 Thomas, *Revelation 8-22,* 331.

252 Kistemaker, *New Testament Commentary,* 494.

253 Thomas, *Revelation 8-22,* 331.

254 Thomas, *Revelation 8-22,* 331-32.

255 Bauckham, *The Climax of Prophecy,* 354.

256 Thomas, *Revelation 8-22,* 332.

the wealthy, imported mostly from Egypt, but also from Spain and Asia Minor.[257] Linen could be symbolized with Rome's economic attractiveness, her commercial intercourse including cooperation with the idolatrous religious structure of the trade system.[258]

*Purple (πορφύρας)*: Purple was another expensive cloth and synonymous with extreme luxury. Some of Rome's purple cloth probably came from the clothing and dyeing industries of Miletus, Thyatira (cf. Acts 16:14), Laodicea and Hierapolis, located in the province of Asia to which John sent Revelation.[259] Purple was an expensive material which symbolizes one of the main commodities of Rome, because of its price, it was used not only as a mark of official status, political or cultic but also by private individuals as a deliberate, conspicuous display of affluence.[260]

*Silk* (σιρικοῦ): Silk was imported at great expense from China, some imported by the overland route through Parthia, most via the ports of northwest India,[261] the name itself was derived from οἰ Εηρες from whom Alexander obtained the fabric when he invaded India.[262] The Romans believe that silk grew on trees and considered nard and silk the most expensive things derived from trees.[263] Silk was so expensive as to be a rare sign of wealth and power.[264]

*Scarlet (κοκκίνο)*: Scarlet cloth was an expensive item; it produced from the berry of the kermes oak and was used to dye the cloth which grew in various parts of Asia Minor.[265] The author may be more concentrated on the clothing industry of his own province in

257 Bauckham, *The Climax of Prophecy*, 354.

258 cf. Beale, *The Book of Revelation*, 909.

259 Thomas, *Revelation 8-22*, 332.

260 Bauckham, *The Climax of Prophecy*, 354.

261 Bauckham, *The Climax of Prophecy*, 354.

262 Thomas, *Revelation 8-22*, 332.

263 Bauckham, *The Climax of Prophecy*, 354. The sumptuary laws of 16 C.E. prohibited the wearing of silk by men, but the extent to which silk became common for both male and female dress is indicated by Josephus' account of Roman soldiers dressed in silk at the triumphs of Vespasian and Titus.

264 Smalley, *The Revelation to John*, 454.

265 Kistemaker, *New Testament Commentary*, 495.

Asia Minor. Trimalchio, (a freedman who has made a fortune from sea-borne commerce, apes the ostentatious symbols of the wealth of the Roman upper classes) who represents the first century Roman rich taken to ludicrous absurdity had cushions with crimson or scarlet stuffing.[266] Rome and her wealth were figuratively pictured as composing her clothing, which consists of four luxurious rich attire material trade products.[267] These materials of rich attire demonstrate the excessive wealth of Rome as well as the luxurious life of the rich elites in Roman society.

## *Materials for Costly Furniture (All Thyine Wood, Every Vessel of Ivory)*

*All Kinds of Scented Wood (πᾶν ξύλον θύϊνον)*: The construction here changes and ξύλον is governed directly by ἀγοράζει. This change may be due not to a slip on the part of the translator, but to a right rendering of his text. The οὐδεὶς ἀγοράζει is to be taken closely with πᾶν ξύλον "no one buy any thyine wood." Hence, καὶ πᾶν ξύλον θύϊνον should be rendered "or any thyine wood."[268] θύϊνον, this wood most probably from *Thuia articulata* of botany, a tree which grew in N. Africa. It was known to the Greeks as θύα, θύον or θύια to the Romans as *citrus*. It was much used in the making of costly tables;[269] Cicero bought such a table and reportedly paid 500,000 sesterces for one table,[270] an amount that was sufficient to purchase a large estate.[271] The colour also varied in different specimens, it was

266 Bauckham, *The Climax of Prophecy*, 356.

267 Beale, *The Book of Revelation*, 911.

268 R. H. Charles, *A Critical and Exegetical Commentary on The Revelation of St. John*, ICC Vol. 2 (Edinburgh: T&T Clark, Reprinted 1959), 103.

269 Charles, *A Critical and Exegetical Commentary on The Revelation*, 103.

270 500,000 sesterces were equal to $2,500,000. Gallus Asinius paid 1,000,000 sesterces ($5,000,000) for another; King Juba of Mauretania auctioned off two such tables, one for 1,200,000 sesterces ($6,000,000) and another for a little less (four sesterces=one denarii, and since one denarius was a labourer's daily wage, then one denarius would roughly equal $40) (Aune, *Revelation 17-22 WBC Vol. 52C*, 1000).

271 Kistemaker, *New Testament Commentary*, 495.

also used for veneering, and for small works of art, which were made out of the hard roots of the tree.[272]

*All Articles of Ivory (ἐλεφάντινον)*: Ivory was imported from Africa and India.[273] The Hebrews used ivory for boxes, beds and even in the building. It is mentioned by Ezekiel (27:15) among the imports of Tyre. By wealthy Romans under the Empire, it was largely used in the decoration of furnitures such as beds, couches, doors, flutes, lyres, combs, brooches, pins, scrapers, boxes, bird-cage, floors, and tables.[274] It is said that 'people cannot enjoy their supper unless their table rests on a leopard carved in ivory.'[275]

*All Articles of Costly Wood (ξύλου τιμιωτάτου), Bronze (χαλκοῦ), Iron (σιδήρου) and Marble (μαρμάρου)*: Costly wood included maple, cedar, cypress, and possibly ebony from Africa and India.[276] In ancient times, bronze as an alloy made of copper and tin was produced in many countries. It was highly prized, and according to Pliny (one ancient writer), it was regarded as even more valuable than silver or gold. Iron deposits in Greece, Spain, and Hungary supplied the Roman world with this metal to fashion tools and weapons. Marble came from Phrygia, Greece, and parts of Africa. It decorated the homes of wealthy citizens.[277] The major marble quarries of the empire were annexed to imperial ownership in the early first century so that they might more efficiently supply the needs of Rome. Pliny treats the private use of marbles as an absurd and indefensible luxury.[278]

### Precious Spices (Cinnamon, Spice, Incense, Myrrh, Frankincense)

καὶ κιννάμωμον καὶ ἄμωμον καὶ θυμιάματα καὶ μύρον καὶ λίβανον (18:13). Among the precious spices, κιννάμωμον, *cinnamon* is of Phoenician origin, but the substance, made from the bark of a tree originated in East Asia or South China. The Phoenicians and

---

272 Swete, *The Apocalypse of St. John,* 233.

273 Aune, *Revelation 17-22 WBC,* 1000.

274 Swete, *The Apocalypse of St. John,* 233; Bauckham, *The Climax of Prophecy,* 357.

275 Swete, *The Apocalypse of St. John,* 233.

276 Thomas, *Revelation 8-22,* 333.

277 Kistemaker, *New Testament Commentary,* 495-96.

278 Bauckham, *The Climax of Prophecy,* 359.

Arabians brought it to Judea. Among the Romans, it was one of the cosmetics of the banquet, used for incense, medicine, perfume, and as a condiment in wines.[279] It was also imported from East Africa, Arabia, and India.[280] *Spice* (ἄμωμον) was imported from south India,[281] *Incense* (θυμιάματα) was an element used for burning in cultic worship,[282] they were expensive aromatic spices and gums when burned, this mixture produced a perfumed smoke that was used not only for religious purposes but also for perfuming the rooms and funerals of the rich.[283] *Myrrh* (μύρον) refers generally to the aromatic ointment, not exclusively to that made from myrrh (σμύρνα), it was imported from Yemen and Somalia at great expense and was certainly one of the most prized of such perfumes.[284] *Frankincense* (λίβανον), like other aromatics, was used as perfumes, imported from Southern Arabia (cf. Isa 60:6; Jer 6:20).[285] All these spices (perfumes/aromatics) were costly and expensive also considered worthy of being presented as gifts to royalty (Matt 2:11).

## Articles of Food (Wine, Olive Oil, Choice Flour and Wheat)

Other categories of the cargoes were food items. These items were the daily staples in most common households. Rome imported *wine* (οἶνον) from Sicily, Spain, and Greece. The Greek recognized three types of wine, the Romans four: white wine (λευκὸς), brown wine (κιρρὸς), and red wine (ἐρυθὸς μέλας), divided by the Romans into light red (*sanguineus*) and dark red (*niger*).[286] Producing wine was very profitable in first century Rome. In fact, the wealthy landowners

279 Thomas, *Revelation 8-22*, 334.

280 Aune, *Revelation 17-22 WBC Vol. 52C*, 1001.

281 Bauckham, *The Climax of Prophecy*, 360.

282 Kistemaker, *New Testament Commentary*, 496.

283 Thomas, *Revelation 8-22*, 334.

284 Bauckham, *The Climax of Prophecy*, 360-61. Pliny asserts that it was one of the expensive feminine, if used by men, effeminate-indulgences which were ruining the society of his time. It was also one of the precious commodities known in Solomon's day too (Prov 7:17; Song 1:13; 3:6; 4:6, 14; 5:1, 5, 13).

285 Bauckham, *The Climax of Prophecy*, 361. They are also kinds of perfumes which were consumed in vast quantities at the funerals of the rich.

286 Aune, *Revelation 17-22 WBC Vol. 52C*, 1002.

quit planting grain and corn and cultivated vines, for this reason, the wine was one of the precious commodities connected with Tyre too (Eze 27:18).[287] *Olive oil* (ἔλαιον) was produced in Italy and imported from North Africa and Spain and were vast quantities of olive oil used in the Roman Empire.[288] *Fine Flour* (σεμίδαλιν) refers to the finest grade of wheaten flour. Not only did the Jews put it to use with wine and incense in their sacrifices (Lev 2:1-2), but Jerusalem also misused it as a delicacy in luxurious living (Eze 16:14).[289] Bauckham remarks that 'although the other three items of food (wine, oil, wheat) grouped together in the list were staples for all inhabitants of Rome, it is noteworthy that the list's general emphasis on luxury is maintained by this reference to fine flour imported for the wealthy.'[290] *Wheat* (σῖτον) was imported by Rome from Alexandria and Africa for the use of her rich. Egypt was the granary for Rome's wheat.[291] Since the Republic of Rome, about 200,000 recipients, i.e., adult males, of the citizen of Rome (population ca. 750,000 to 1,000,000) had been provided with the free distribution of grain i.e., 80,000 tons of grain annually. It took thousands of ships to import the required amount of grain to Rome.[292] This certainly portrays the wealth and luxurious life of the Roman Empire. The above articles of food demonstrate the economic background of Rome/Revelation, storage and a shortage of the most basic foodstuff, a city of a million people[293] - the largest city in the western world could not have grown and survived without the sufficient supply of this basic foodstuff. These are the staple foods in those times rather than luxuries, and it

287 Thomas, *Revelation 8-22,* 334.

288 Thomas, *Revelation 8-22,* 334.

289 Thomas, *Revelation 8-22,* 334.

290 Bauckham, *The Climax of Prophecy,* 362.

291 Charles, *A Critical and Exegetical Commentary on The Revelation,* 104.

292 Aune, *Revelation 17-22 WBC Vol. 52C,* 1002.

293 The size of the first-century Rome's population was estimated at 800,000 to one million (See G. Rickman, "The Grain Trade Under the Roman Empire," in J. H. D'Arms and E. C. Kopff eds., *The Seabourne Commerce of Ancient Rome: Studies in Archaeology and History* (Memoirs of the American Academy in Rome 36; Rome: American Academy in Rome, 1980), 261-176.

is certain that they would have made them extremely profitable in trade systems that also shows the economic wealth of Rome.

### *Merchandised for Agricultural and Domestic uses (Cattle, Sheep, Horses and Chariots)*

This section illustrates the agricultural and domestic wealth/ dimensions of the image of the Roman Empire. Imports of animals to Rome is not easy, it should have shown that the methods of transporting livestock in ships in the imperial period must have been well developed. *Cattle* (κτήνη) *and sheep* (πρόβατα), κτήνη means all kinds of cattle for drought or riding.[294] The Roman aristocracy had acquired large sheep and cattle ranches both in Italy and in the provinces through conquest and confiscation[295] that also focuses on the wealth of Rome.

### *Traffic in Human (Slaves, Human Lives)*

The insidious nature of imperial trade is underscored by the commodities that conclude the list "bodies and human souls" (18:13) which signifies slaves.[296] In ancient Rome, slaves have commonly labelled "bodies." They were not considered human beings but commodities that could be bought and sold, so, within the Roman Empire, everyone can become a commodity. There are various sources of slaves like wars, offspring of existing slaves, foundlings, children sold by their parents, adults selling themselves into slavery,

294 Charles, *A Critical and Exegetical Commentary on The Revelation,* 104. The OT sees cattle as a sign of wealth too (Ps 50:10; 1 Sam 25:2), the import of sheep was probably not for food but for breeding purposes, to improve the quality of Roman wool. Scholars like V. M. Scramuzza believe that the import of sheep from Sicily was for the meat for the rich people (See Bauckham, *The Climax of Prophecy*, 364).

295 Thomas, *Revelation 8-22*, 335. *Horses and chariots* (i[ppwn kai. r`edw/n), racehorses for chariot racing in the circuses were imported from Africa, Spain, Sicily, Cappadocia and parts of Greece famous for their horses (Laconia, Thessalia, Aetolia). *Chariots* (r`edw/n), Latin *raeda* or *reda*, were the four-wheeled vehicle in which the Roman aristocracy rode, horse-drawn, private chariots used by the rich for travel in Rome and to their country estates. (See Bauckham, *The Climax of Prophecy*, 364).

296 Howard-Brook, *Unveiling Empire,* 173.

slavery through debt, victims of kidnapping, some criminals etc. With regard to the question of Revelation using the term of a slave, the noun *σωμάτων* continues the series of genitives of which it is the last member and the expression *ψυχὰς ἀνθρώπων* returns to the accusative case, directly dependent on *ἀγοράζει* of v. 11. Some have cited the difference in a case as a reason for understanding two groups of human merchandise: slaves connected with the horses and chariots just mentioned (*σωμάτων*) and slaves in general (*ψυχὰς ἀνθρώπων*). The term *σωμάτων* is a shortened way of writing *σωμάτων δοὺλων* or *σωμάτων οἰκετικων*. In Gen 34:29 of the LXX *σωμάτων* refers to slaves. A slave merchant was called *σωμάτεμπορος*. In Gen 36.6 Esau left Canaan with his wives, sons, daughters, and all the *σωμάτα τοὺ οἰκου αυτοὺ* – his slaves (cf. Tob 10:10; Bel 32:2 Macc 8:11). Sweet notes that *slaves* came early in Ezekiel's list (27:13), but here they came at the end of a list which is in descending order of value or the placement could be for rhetorical effect. For a good discussion on the list of cargoes as Bauckham noted. Earlier he notes that it is no accident that the list comprises twenty-eight items because 4 (the number of the world) times 7 (the number of completeness) equals 28, making the list representatives of all the products of the whole world. He also holds that the final clause, being in an emphatic position, is a comment on the entire list of cargoes. It suggests the inhuman brutality, the contempt for human life, on which the whole of Rome's prosperity and luxury rests. Bengel suggests that the bodies are slaves used for carrying goods and the souls of men are slaves considered as merchandise, which has the advantage of linking swma,twn with the genitives that precede it and allowing the awkward shift to the accusative *ψυχὰς*.[297] This particular verse -18:13 (καὶ σωμάτων, καὶ ψυχὰς ἀνθρώπω) translated differently "and slaves, that is, human souls" (RSV); "and bodies and souls of men" (NIV); "slaves, and even human lives" (TEV), despite the variation of translation, the main focus of here is no other than slaves. Increasing

297 Robert H. Mounce, *The Book of Revelation NICNT* Cambridge: Eerdmans Publishing Company, 1977, 334; Henry Alfrod, *The Greek Testament.* London: Longmans, Green, 1903, 718.

numbers of *slaves* (σωμάτων) in Rome were a feature of the growing prosperity of the rich and the increasing size of the city.[298]

The usage of the term in Revelation may have variation interpretation. Rhetorically, there were precedents for using the term "slave" in a positive sense for those who are devoted to God. In Israel's tradition, Moses and other prophets were given the honourable title "slave of God." Revelation reflects this usage (10:7; 15:3) and extends it by giving the honorific title of "slave" to a Christian prophet like John. There were also precedents for calling any faithful person in Israel a slave of God (Ps 27:9; 2 Chr 6:23), and Revelation also uses the term for each member of the Christian community (2:20; 19:2; 22:6). This pattern was not unusual. Similar uses of the word "slave" for those devoted to God occur in other early Christian writings as well as in Greco-Roman sources. In NT, in Pauline slavery, the metaphor of slavery shaped Pauline theology, Paul calls himself a "slave of Christ," an apostolic designation (Rom 1:1; Phil 1:1; Gal 1:10) and the slave of all a common place trope of servant leadership (1 Cor 3:5; 9:19-23; 2 Cor 4:5). Paul arguably accepts and even encourages the manumission of (urban) slaves. The Apostle's acceptance of manumission is not a cry for abolitionism, however. By incorporating the Roman institutionalized practices of manumission into his theology. Paul speaks in ways similar to other Greco-Roman connected to slave ownership social conservatism (and support of slavery) in the Greco-Roman world did not include the restriction of manumission.[299]

The term for slaves is literally "bodies" (σώματα). This term could be used for any enslaved person, but it is especially suitable for a context in which slaves are regarded as a commodity. Those captured in war could be put on the slave market as "bodies" (2 Macc 8:11). Traders would travel by land and sea looking for "bodies" to buy so that they could resell them at a profit in slave markets elsewhere. It cannot be denied that slavery could not be abandoned since it became part of the culture in the early centuries, not only

298 Bauckham, *The Climax of Prophecy,* 365.

299 Craig R. Koester, "Roman Slave Trade and the Critique of Babylon in Revelation 18" *CBQ* 70 (2008), 765-786

in terms of economic, but society also demanded.[300] 'Slave society' is very common and slavery is fully commercialized in the in the Roman Empire. While Slavery was an essential component of the social life of Rome both in economic and political; but, at the same time, the Roman usage of 'slaves' found in Revelation (18:13) is a terminology of dehumanization, to treat them as objects without life and soul is sufficient proof for Rome's anti-God and anti-human approach. Thus, the merchant destroys their own humanity as well as the humanity of the slaves.[301]

In any case, slave trading was a profitable business, and Asia Minor was evidently the most important source of those slaves who were not taken in war. Ephesus, an important city played a major role in exporting slaves from Asia Minor to Rome.[302] The whole of the Roman economy, not just the agrarian part, depended on slave labour.[303] The number of slaves in the Roman Empire in the first century C.E. has been estimated at around 10,000,000, which is 16.6 percent to 20 percent of the population, the majority of whom were male.[304] Robert Mounce also asserts that there were 60,000,000 estimated slaves in the Roman Empire.[305] The slave trade was a trademark of Roman commerce in Asia Minor and Rome became the greatest of all slave markets in those days.

### *Comments*

The above study clearly pictured the economic wealth of the Roman Empire. Looking all the list of the cargoes and the destruction of the city, it is not only the city of Rome who commits economic sin but also her colleagues and economic partner, who was involved in Rome's economic sin. Behind the list of cargoes and its destruction, it can be seen that the luxurious life of the Roman ruling elites in

---

300 J. Albert Harrill, "Slavery" *NIDB*: 299-308.

301 M. M.Thomas, *The Revelation to John*. Translated by T. M. Philip. (Tiruvala: CSS Books, 2014), 153.

302 Bauckham, *The Climax of Prophecy*, 366.

303 Ben Witherington III, *Revelation*, 228.

304 Aune, *Revelation 17-22 WBC*, 1003.

305 Mounce, *The Book of Revelation*, 334.

those days. Their wealth is beyond measure, their trade is global worldwide and their economic status was also reaching its peak.

The historical proof of the wealth of Rome was found in the second century, a considerable amount of goods from the empire-expensive glass and drinking cups of silver, plainer buckets and cauldrons-was reaching not only Denmark but Norway and Sweden also, and the weight system used during the Iron Age in Norway was based upon the Roman *denarius*.[306] While the wealthy ruling elite enjoys their luxurious life, the poor and the peasants were oppressed and exploited in the name of economic development. Bauckham remarks that John sees a connection between Rome's economic affluence, Rome's idolatrous self-deification, and Rome's military and political brutality.[307] While the list of the cargoes is the evidence of the conspicuous wealth and extravagance of the rich families of Rome, the image behind the list of cargoes also proved economic exploitation and unjust system/structure.

## 4.7. The Final Judgment of Economic Rome: 18:20-24

### *Introduction*

The previous passage portrays the destruction of the objects, but in this passage, the destruction of the persecutor, the ruling elites, the collaborators of Rome, the one who constantly tried to seduce them into idolatry and other sins, has been displayed. This passage reminds us that God's authoritative judgment by saying the echoes of OT concept 'vengeance is mine' says the LORD (Deut 32:35 OT) which was repeated in NT Romans 12:19 ("vengeance is mine, I will repay, says the Lord"), and it also portrays the sovereign authority of God that no one can challenge it.

### *Exegetical Notes*

The catastrophe of Babylon and her allies was viewed by M. M. Thomas in employing two aspects: on the one hand, the creative powers, the Creator's gift to the humans stands at the base of any

306 M. P. Charlesworth, *The Roman Empire* (Reprinted; London: Oxford University Press, 1961), 131.

307 Bauckham, *The Climax of Prophecy*, 349-50.

culture. On the other hand, because of human pride human creative powers have turned destructive and that also is evident in a culture, and because of this destructiveness divine punishment has become inevitable, thus, along with the lament over the fall, justification is also seen alongside.[308] Verse 20 says that heaven and saints, apostles, and prophets are called upon to rejoice over the demise of Babylon. The bad news for the oppressor is the good news for the oppressed.[309] The involvement of heaven (οὐρανε) in this song (v. 20) is reminiscent of Jer 51:48-49, another song of joy over the demise of Babylon. The vocative οὐρανε changes the mood of singing from lamentation to that of gaiety. The same thing that causes deep sorrow on earth brings great jubilation to heaven.[310] Verse 20 forms a triumphant conclusion to the dreary scene of Babylon's fall, which could not be concluded without a joyful response of the martyrs. Here, God heard the plea and cries of the by the margins, poor and economically the oppressed under the Roman Imperialism and adjourned with a final judgment.

In v. 21, a strong angel who takes a millstone and cast into the sea symbolizing the fall of Babylon and picturing the sinking of the great city of Rome and also symbolizes the complete destruction and disappearance of Rome.[311] The judgment of God is strong and beyond challenged for the great empire of Rome. This is the fate of the city of Babylon. The passage reminds the reader of Jeremiah 51:63-64 when Jeremiah took a scroll and wrote out on it all the judgment that would befall Babylon. An angelic solo in v. 21 follows these mournful choruses, a dirge of Babylon's sudden and fatal demise. Her destruction is swift, as the prophetic gesture of the plummeting millstone and its watery burial suggest. Her destruction is permanent, as the emphatic double negations in the Greek insist: in vv. 22 and 23 the double negative construction is repeated no less

---

308 Thomas, *The Revelation to John,* 154-55.

309 Ben Witherington III, *Revelation*, 230.

310 Thomas, *Revelation 8-22,* 341.

311 E. H. M. Waller, *The Revelation of St. John the Divine with Introduction and Notes* (Madras: London SPCK, 1926), 348.

than six times[312] which signifies the affirmative of divine punishment because the destruction of Rome brings both challenge and judgment.

The prophets and saints (people of God) προφητῶν καὶ ἁγίων included all the oppressed and marginalized victims of economic injustice, while the parallel line 'those slain on the earth' may also refer to all those who are put to death due to economic exploitation and victims of economic capitalism by Babylon-Rome. This final passage affirmed that the guilt of Rome was unable to forgiven and sin against God.

## *Comments*

This passage (vv. 20-24) portrayed the final judgment upon economic Rome. The economic crime of Rome against the divine nature must be punished or destroy from the sight of the author (seer). Thus, it was happened in various manners in accordance to destroy the strong point of unjust economic Rome. All the pride and symbols of mighty Rome- the great sound of violence was sunk at the sea, the melodious of all musical echoes were shut down, all the luxurious trades of artistic skills were bent down, the joy of light and the joyful sound of marriages and happiest moments of occasions were gone. This shows that the strength of Rome was defeated. All the pride pillars and

312 Allen D. Callahan, "Apocalypse as Critique of Political Economy: Some Notes on Revelation 18" in *HBT* Vol. 21 (1999): 46-65. The double negation *οὐ μὴ ωιτη ἔτι* "no more." In powerful poetic verse, John envisions everything as lost (vv.22-23), the sound of harpist and minstrels, of flautists and trumpet players- no more; craftspeople of any craft- no more; the sound of the millstone-no more; the light of the lamp- no more; the voice of the bridegroom- no more; everything that humanizes civilization like music, art, industry, light, love are all perished and gone. The *angelus interpres* gives the reader a graphic account of the sentence executed upon the Great City and delineates the capital offenses of which she has been convicted. Domination by commercial agents, the tyranny of the class with cash, is an offense against God, and so God has found Babylon guilty on all counts. On the charge of investing mercantile moguls with greatness: guilty. On the charge of poisoning the international community, farmakeia-*pharmakeia*- a narcotics charge: guilty. On the charge of the global murder of innocent people: guilty. Babylon's realm is a world empire, and so Babylon's slaughter and conspiracy are worldwide. It is an empire that slaughters not only the prophets and saints but *πάντων τῶν ἐσφαγμένων ἐπὶ τῆς γῆς* "all the earth who have been slaughtered" (Rev 18:24).

glory of Rome was demolished because as the author remarks that the corrupt rulers of merchants and the magical sorcery of the city that misled all the nations cause this doomsday. The shedding blood of the oppressed and the marginalized causes the final judgment of Rome. This clearly demonstrates that economic sin is against God and was unforgiving.

## 4.8. Conclusion

The above research clearly depicts the inner wealth and luxurious lives of Rome, and, the rhetorical reading with post-colonial lens of apocalypse coherent the reality of the unjust economic empire. While the list of cargoes symbolizes the wealth of Rome, it also depicts the imbalanced of economic prosperity in the empire; the reaction of the mourners of the fall of Rome signifies their selfish human nature since they mourn only over their own economic demise and loss of their cargoes by exempting the pity of the people. It also depicted their corrupted mind. The detailed study of the text reminds that the sins of Rome is basically rooted in the economic injustice which is a serious crime against God, because of the unjust economic activities, the entire system, its coercive and seductive powers of Rome was completely annihilated. Critically looking the whole drama of the final judgment of Rome, it portrays that human culture is materialized through the development of God-given talents and abilities, the misuse of human creative powers which it turned into destruction. M. M. Thomas rightly viewed that this economic injustice or the misuse of merchandised effects to the creative power of those involved in economic activities, and should be noted that if those who handle money get greater importance than those who give cultural leadership then deterioration of values will be faster.[313] Therefore, this research proves that economic injustice becomes a centre of the fall of Babylon (Rome).

313 Thomas, *The Revelation to John*, 155-56.

Chapter 5

# A Critique of Economic Capitalism in Roman Imperialism It's Implication for Today's Context

## 5.1 Introduction

This chapter deals with the critical appraisal of Roman Economic system and the practice of Capitalism which became economic guilt that discriminating the society into two big groups as the wealthy and the poor class (peasant-slave) people, and also misuse of money power and exercising the authority against the poor, the oppressed and the marginalized. The research also deals about Babylonialism today like money worship, corruption, economic injustice and so on. In the book of Revelation, the economic condemnation of Rome is the most unusual aspect of the opposition of Rome. While discussing the unjust economic issues of Rome, the contextual relevancy of the issue also employed and the same scenario of Roman economic exploitation is seen in our present context which is addressed in this chapter.

## 5.2. Brief Survey of the Roman Trade

Roman trade was worldwide in the early centuries and became the engine that drove the Roman economy. Perhaps because of the trade, language and legions were also became the backbone of Rome which lasted the Roman Empire for making a strong and prosperous empire. The global marketing of Rome was stretching from Rome to Britain and Syria, from Britain to Greece and Egypt, and from Spain and North Africa to Rome, and in the east to India and China.[314] Rev 18:12-13 also mentioned the lists of cargoes which imported from different parts of the world showed the global business trade of Rome. Bauckham remarks that it was the wealth of her subjects she squandered on the extravagant luxuries listed in these verses.[315]

The eulogy of the great commerce of Rome in the second century was also mentioned by Greek rhetorician Aelius Aristides in his message of 'In Praise of Rome 200-201'[316] which clearly pictured the trade and commerce of Rome. The Roman period also witnessed the extension of Near Eastern and Hellenistic features such as urbanization, monetization, market exchange, taxation, and chattel slavery into the western peripheries of Eurasia.[317] In addition to this, the list of cargoes mentioned in Rev 18:12-13 confirms the global trade of Rome. It is not surprising that several of the items belong wholly or partly to the eastern trade with Arabia, East Africa, and India and beyond, which flourished especially under the early

---

314 Shelton, *As the Romans Did-A Source Book in Roman Social History*, 135.

315 Richard Bauckham, *The Bible in Politics-How to read the Bible Politically* (Britain: SPCK, 1989), 94.

316 Aristides message describe the Roman Trade as: "Large continents lie all around the Mediterranean and from them to you, flow constant supplies of goods. Everything is shipped to you, from every land and every sea-the products of each season, of each country, of each river and lakes, the craft of Greeks and other foreigners. As a result, if anyone wants to see all these items, he must either travel through the whole world to behold them or live in this city of Rome." (See Shelton, *As the Romans Did-A Source Book in Roman Social History*, 136).

317 Walter Scheidel ed., *The Cambridge Companion to the Roman Economy* (Cambridge: Cambridge University Press, 2012), 1. Scheidel further states that there are three necessary things to understand Roman Economic history: 1) determine what happened, 2) explain why it happened, and 3) access these developments comparatively by relating them to those of other times and places, thereby situating the Roman case in a global context of pre-modern economic performance.

empire.[318] In such a wealthy economic trade of Rome, it has to be noted that the ruling elites were the prime advantage to get a profit while the farmers and peasants were not able to enjoy the wealth of Rome. So, it is important to understand that in Roman society participants in the 'cash economy' – those who had access to free cash and who could, therefore, take part in the commodity marker were very few in number.[319] Therefore, the apocalypse affirmed that while the right hand was holding the Roman coin, the empire would transfix the mind of the bearer.

## *The Great Trade of Rome*

In the Roman trade, everything that is grown or manufactured by each people is not only always present here but is present in abundance. So, many ships land in Rome bringing cargo from all over, during every season, after every harvest. And thus, the city seems like a common market for the world.[320] Many cargoes imported from India, clothing from Babylonia and ornaments from foreign lands beyond arrive at Rome in greater quantity and more easily than goods shipped from Naxos or Cythos[321] to Athens. Egypt, Sicily, and the cultivated part of Lybia are the farms. The arrival and departure of ships never cease. And consequently, it is quite amazing that there is enough room in the sea, much less the harbour, for the ships…Everything comes from together here: trade and commerce, the transportation industry, agriculture, metallurgy, every skill which exists now and has existed, all that is produced and grows.[322]

## *Usage of Coins in the Roman Market Economy*

In the Roman market economy, tenants paid rent on their apartments in Rome; employers paid wages to free workers and rent for slaves, travelers paid for food and drinks for themselves and their animals. These are the ordinary prices of a market economy, showing that

318 Bauckham, *The Climax of Prophecy*, 367.

319 Douglas E. Oakman, "The Ancient Economy and St. John's Apocalypse," *Listening* 28 (1993), 200-214.

320 Shelton, *As the Romans Did-A Source Book in Roman Social History*, 136.

321 Naxos, Cythos: Greek Islands in the Aegean.

322 Shelton, *As the Romans Did-A Source Book in Roman Social History*, 136.

many of the goods and services used in the course of ordinary life were valued by price and paid for by money.[323] These payments made coin available in those days. The abundant evidence of Roman coinage testifies to the common use of coins as a means of payment. A coin was used for transactions throughout the Roman Empire. It seems obvious that they carried a coin in anticipation of spending their money buying goods and services in market exchange.[324] While mentioning money/coins, the loan system already introduces in Roman Economy too.[325]

There are many records of loans in Roman economy, among which in 141 C.E. a woman loaned 3,500 drachmae to another woman in Egypt for one year at the same interest rate, 420 drachmae for a one-year loan, by a draft on a private bank. The interest rate was almost always in the range of four to twelve percent, seldom higher than the rate in these provincial loans. This range may reflect a prohibition on loans at more than twelve percent. Money lending was as common in ancient Rome as it is today. Today, however, most people borrow large sums of money from a bank or savings and loan institution; in ancient Rome, "bankers" were private individuals with enough capital to make loans. And, despite Cicero's denigration of money lending, some of the "best" people made their fortunes by lending money, although they may have concealed the fact by using agents.

In Revelation 18, the author also warns the threat of money power under the Roman imperialism, he warns his audience about the danger of getting into bed economically with the emperor and empire by telling a tale of two cities: Rome and the New Jerusalem. He serves up a rhetorical comparison, by contrast, meant to help his audience disengage and disentangle themselves from the idolatrous economics of the emperor cult.[326] He urged and warns them not

323 Peter Temin, "A Market Economy in the Early Roman Empire," *JRS* Vol. 91 (2001), 169-181.

324 Temin, "A Market Economy in the Early Roman Empire," 174.

325 Shelton, *As the Romans Did-A Source Book in Roman Social History,*136; J. Rowlandson, *Women and Society in Greek and Roman Egypt.* (Cambridge: Cambridge University Press, 1998), 254-5.

326 Ben Witherington III, *Jesus & Money* (Great Britain: SPCK, 2010), 135.

to imprison themselves into the unclean Roman economy *vis-à-vis* money power.

To some extent, in relation to coins[327] and power, J. David Singer observed that power is to us what money is to the economist: the medium via which transactions are observed and measured.[328] Moreover, as Pyung Soo Seo rightly pointed out that coin-minting it frequently implies a ruler's authority in the ancient world. There are various examples of direct links between coin-minting and one's authority. All too often, the rulers are shown on the coins in order to express their authority/power. Thus, the head of the emperor on the imperial coins was viewed as a symbol of authority.[329] More importantly, the emperors often issued the coins during their reign to highlight their authority by linking it to their control of minting.[330] Therefore, it is clear that imperial coinage represents the emperor's supreme authority in the empire; a symbol/image of the emperor on the coins signifies the supreme authority/power of the emperor.

## 5.3. What is Economic Capitalism?

Capitalism is an economic system where private sectors are allowed to own and control the use of property in accord with their own interests. Under capitalism, ownership of the means of production is vested in one set of individuals while the work is performed by another. Both means of production and labour power, moreover, are commodities; that is to say, both are objects of exchange and hence bearers of exchange value. It may, therefore, say that the buying and

---

327 During the early Roman period coins circulating in Israel came from three main sources: The Roman coins minted according to the imperial standard; the provincial coins minted at Antioch and Tyre; and local coinages minted by local governors and procurators, and the Herodians. The different standards, as well as the restrictions on money the Temple would accept. Necessitated the money-changers controlled daily exchange rates, as well as discounted and recycled worn coinage (Gerald M. Bikes "Money, Coins" *NIDB*: 130-137.

328 J. David Singer, "Inter-Nation Influence: A Formal Model," *APSR*, 57 (June 1963): 420.

329 Seo, *Luke's Jesus in the Roman Empire and the Emperor in the Gospel of Luke*, 59.

330 Seo, *Luke's Jesus in the Roman Empire and the Emperor in the Gospel of Luke*, 60.

selling of labour power is the *differentia specifica* of capitalism.[331] In describing the nature of Capitalism, Karl Marx looked forward to a new manifestation of the forces of human nature and a new enrichment of human nature was scathing in his denunciation of artificial stimulation of consumption.[332]

In other words, the term Capitalism used to mean the creation of business (entrepreneurship) combined with the benefits of competition (free enterprise, the market system) with the profits going to the entrepreneur and the investors. The classic definition of capitalism was "the private ownership of the means of production."[333] The broader understanding of capitalism has been developed as Capitalism is not simply an economic system, however; it is also a state of mind, an attitude[334] that controls all the power of economics and misuses the authority that affects the basic necessity of the country

---

331 Paul M. Sweezy, *The Theory of Capitalist Development* (New Delhi: KP Bagchi & Company, 1991), 56.

332 Ajit Roy, *On Marxist Theory and Practice: From Stalin and Mao to Gorbachev and Deng* (Calcutta: The Marxist Review Publications, 1992), 48. Karl Marx opines that 'under capitalism, every person speculates on creating a new need in another, so as to drive him to a fresh sacrifice, to place him in a new dependence and to seduce him into a new mode of gratification and therefore economic ruin. The increase in the number of objects is accompanied by an extension of the realm of alien powers to which man is subjected. Man becomes ever poorer as a man his neediness grows as the power of money increases.'

333 Arthur Jones, *Capitalism and Christians-Through Gospel Challenges in a Troubled World Economy* (New York: Paulist Press, 1992), 5. He further states that the traditional understanding of Capitalism was developed and now used and can be best understood as one word describing three states of economic activity: capitalism the good, capitalism the bad, and capitalism the ugly. *Capitalism the good (Business):* Ignition-the entrepreneurial stage that creates wealth where none existed by teaming together ideas, capital, and human energy. The beneficial-the newly freed wealth creates jobs and income for the community. Business is every commercial enterprise honestly run, from the corner store to major hotel to International Corporation, in which the human element takes equal place to the need for the profits that ensure survival. *Capitalism the bad*: This is both a stage and the process of business being corrupted. It may create jobs for some and profits for others, but someone is going to suffer as profits are maximized.

334 Jones, *Capitalism and Christians,* 9.

and her citizens in a negative sense. The real picture of capitalism is seen in the Roman Economy, the ruling elites misled the good economic capitalism to the ugly capitalism by exercising their power against the poor, peasant, subaltern and the marginalized.

The reality of capitalism is much broader and more troublesome than its ideologues allow. Its islands of wealth are set in seas of poverty. Given the immense economic misery which exists amidst plenty, the huge military expenditure that governments of the world still feel obliged to make and the terrible environmental destruction, the most important questions are not related to the narrow "contest" between centralized socialist countries and the capitalist countries.[335] Thus, capitalism became the dominant economic system. Capitalism is also sometimes called the private enterprise system,[336] so as Capitalism

---

335 Arjun Makhikani, *From Global Capitalism to Economic Justice* (New York: The Apex Press, 1992), 5. Arjun further describe the effects of economic capitalism as: Despite the fact that we live in a world which is only a few minutes away from the threat of a total destruction by nuclear war, governments still spend a trillions of dollars a year on the production, deployment and use of armaments that could trigger a nuclear war; 12-15 million children die every year of malnutrition and easily preventable disease, amelioration of which would require resources amounting to no more than those spent on armaments in a week or two; because of the economic system values only that which has a monetary price, nurture as well as nature ate effectively excluded from the economic calculus; the economic system disconnects the humanity of producers from that of consumers, so that price, value, and quality of goods are separated from the conditions under which the producers must labour to produce goods as well as from the environmental consequences of production. This is particularly true of production for export in the Third world; the economic system subordinates product safety and product quality to considerations such as profit.

336 Wayne A. Leeman, *Capitalism, Market Socialism and Central Planning* (Delhi: Khosla & Co., 1976), 3. Milton Friedman opines that the development of capitalism has been accompanied by a major reduction in the extent to which particular religious, racial, or social groups have operated under special handicaps in respect of their economic activities; have, as saying goes, been discriminated against. Furthermore, Tamas Szentes also asserts that Capitalism as a social system has in general introduced economic coercion as the method for appropriating surplus. Its history is the process by which monopolistic private ownership, which was originally established by non-economic force and which succeeded in excluding the majority of working people from the

focuses on the profit of the investor or the entrepreneur despite the profit of the whole community, it has been rigid to the small ruling elites and it automatically practiced discrimination between the two parties of the investor/entrepreneur and the customers/common citizens.

Revelation 18 talks about Roman capitalism in an apocalyptic manner, it is a remarkable display of rhetorical power, meant to send chills down the spine of anyone who would sell their soul for profits and success, especially by means of government contracts, so to speak. It turns out that not just the kings of the earth but the merchants, the sea captains, and the sailors had all gotten on board the good ship Rome.[337] The Roman Empire, like various modern ones, believed that bigger is better, that more impressive means more important, and that 'succeeding' cures all ills. And it made the huge mistake of a wedding the socio-economic system to both the political and religious systems. It was literally one-stop shopping: worship the emperor and respect the empire, get favourable trade agreements, and prosper.[338] But, the economic mistake of Rome led to the whole destruction of the city.

## 5.4. A Critique of Capitalism in Roman Economy

Roman society was built on a pyramid of patron-client relationships. A person of higher standing (patron) could offer financial assistance or legal protection (patronage) to a person of lower standing (client). By accepting assistance, the client was obligated to offer respect and loyalty to the patron. These relationships existed at the level of the individual, the household, the city, and the province. The emperor was the patron par excellence, and the peoples of the empire are his clients.[339] Warren Carter said that a few people of 2-3% are holding

---

property, eventually came to dominate the main means of production. (See Milton Friedman, *Capitalism and Freedom*. Chicago: The University of Chicago Press, 1982. 108; Tamas Szentes, *The Transformation, Market Socialism and Central Planning*. Delhi: Khosla & Co, 1976. 3).

337 Witherington III, *Jesus & Money*, 136.

338 Witherington III, *Jesus & Money*, 136.

339 Howard-Brook, *Unveiling Empire,* 95.

leadership/authority upon religion, military, and politics.[340] But, Meek believed that authority was at the hand of only 1% of the population.[341] It is clear that power and authority were at the hand of only a few rich elites and high-class people.

In Revelation, the great Roman Economy was marked by illicit economic activity within the larger context of Rome's imperial rule secured by military power and religious practices. Revelation 18 emphasizes the economic extravagance with the idolatrous self-glorification of religious observance and the political control of an eternal empire.[342] The corresponding chapters of Revelation 17 and 18 shows the relation of Roman wealth to Roman rule, Revelation 18 exposes the web of commercial relations in which these political powers provincial regimes that constitute Roman imperial politics are entangled. The κριμα (*krima*-the crime) of this alliance (17:1) calls for the κρισις (*krisis*), the judgment of God (18:10).[343] The list of traded goods in 18:12-13 defines the economic exploitation of Rome and the list represents losses from provinces and often the labour of numerous provincials who received minimal compensation.[344]

Carter again remarks this unjust economy of Rome by stating that accordingly, the wealth and powerful enjoyed an abundant and diverse food supply that divided elites from non-elites.[345] Finley also

---

340 Warren Carter, *Matthew and Empire: Initial Exploration* (Harrisburg: Trinity Press International, 2001), 18.

341 Wayne A. Meeks, *The First Urban Christians: The Social World of the Apostle Paul* (London: Yale University Press, 1983), 53.

342 Carter, *The Roman Empire and the New Testament,* 105-106. In addition to this, Richard Horsley opines that like the modern Mafia, Romans apparently viewed their relationship with other peoples in terms of competition for honour. Rome asserted its superiority by humiliating its enemies, especially those who were far off, exotic, and strange. In the submission, the people had to render up production of their products to their superior conquerors, and it is impossible to separate the economic benefits of imperial domination from the symbolic value of domination and subjugation. (See Richard Horsley, *Jesus and Empire.* Minneapolis: Fortress Press, 2003, 30).

343 Allen D. Callahan, "Apocalypse as Critique of Political Economy: Some notes on Revelation 18," *HBT* 21 No. 1 (Jun 1999), 46-65.

344 Carter, *The Roman Empire and the New Testament,* 108.

345 Carter, *The Roman Empire and the New Testament,* 110

opines that while Rome peaks its empire in economic prosperity, developing the trade system and production, he found that the interest of trade policy is in favour of the ruling elites and the interest for themselves only.[346] He further mentions that the real picture of the Roman economy as-the commercial exchange of goods for private profit was common and requires no demonstration. Trade in agricultural products dominated the scene. How otherwise would landed magnates have acquired their large cash income? The growing Roman Empire, at any rate, stimulated a continuous and substantial increase in the total volume of trade, by the opening up and urbanization of extensive underdeveloped regions; by the tremendous leap in the standard of living and therefore the consumer demands of the upper classes. Successful empire, in sum, benefited trade in general, in ways that he has just indicated briefly. But, whose trade? If we put aside food supply for domestic consumption, not trade- He can find no trace of policy in favour of, or even in the interest of, trading members of the imperial state as against other traders, or in the interest of traders as such, regardless of origin. There were no embargoes, no navigation acts, and no protectionist measures.[347] The theme of the wealth and luxury of Rome (Babylon) is reiterated throughout chapter 18 (vv. 3, 9, 12-15, 16-17 and 19). Although, Rome (Babylon) is accused of luxury and seduction, the indictment extends beyond the city itself to the kings that lived in luxury with her and further to the merchants and mariners who have profited from her.[348] The focus of Rome's luxury is most sharp and explicit in the 28-item list of cargo goods mourned by the merchants.

A political economist Immanuel Wallerstein described the Roman economy consists of one economy (as a single division of labour), one polity, and the ruling groups pressed the direct producers to produce

346 M. I. Finley, "Empire in the Greco Roman World," *Greece and Rome* Vol. 25, No. 1 (Apr 1978): 8.

347 Finley, "Empire in the Greco Roman World," *Greece and Rome* Vol. 25, No. 1 (Apr. 1978), 11-12.

348 Peter S. Perry, "Critiquing the Excess of Empire: A Synkrisis of John of Patmos and Dio of Prusa" *JSNT* 29.4 (2007), 473-496.

a specified surplus over their own direct consumption needs.[349] Allen D. Callahan also comments the unjust political economy of Rome as in Babylon; both treacheries of international real politic and the predation of global commerce are realized together in systematic relation to each other. Israel's political memory of this archetype monument of global hegemony, a synthesis of political and economic domination, provides the biblical trope for the seer's condemnation of Rome.[350] The political unjust economy of Rome is clearly shown by the wealth of Rome and the real picture of the inhabitants (the poor and the peasants) was displayed, oppressed and dominated by the economic power. While the ruling elites celebrate the free trade zones opened all around the Mediterranean and the shippers sing with their cargoes, but on the other side, they oppressed the poor and the marginalized by their wealth and treasury.

Revelation 18 pictured the more victims of the destruction are the kings of the earth, the merchants of the earth and the Mariners (18:3) because they are the ones who enjoy the wealth of Rome. Even when the whole destruction of the city comes, they didn't have the sympathy of the city, rather they weep for their self-pity for losing their best customers and items. This clearly pictures that the economy was not in a balance at its best.

Their luxurious lifestyle (18:12-13) portrays a clear picture of money worship in those days. Money worship *vis-à-vis* power worship creates misuse of power and implemented corruption. This unjust economic capitalism led to the destruction of the Empire. While praising the Roman peace as a symbol of integrity and development of trade route, Bauckham criticised *Pax Romana* as the intoxicating wine from the harlot's cup which was the people's sense of gratitude to the Emperor, who was worshipped as a divine saviour for the blessing he had brought to his subjects.[351]

Capitalism as a social system has in general introduced economic coercion as the method for appropriating surplus, the capitalist system

349 Immanuel Wallerstein, *The Politics of World Economy* (London: Cambridge University Press, 1984), 150-151.

350 Allen D. Callahan, "Apocalypse as Critique of Political Economy: Some Notes on Revelation 18." *HBT* Vol. 21 (1999), 46-65.

351 Bauckham, *The Bible in Politics,* 91.

was built on the appropriation of the surplus product of labour[352] and the profit goes to the owner or ruling elites. Mohan Razu opines that the present system of global economic governance is premised on capitalistic principles. The multilateral global institutions play as instruments to preserved and promote the hegemony of the system of global capitalism and thus benefit from this arrangement.[353] Thus, the same scenario is found in Roman imperialism as global capitalism is tearing down all non-market structures that placed a limitation on the accumulation and the dictatorship of capital. Therefore, it can be assumed that the same image of Roman economic capitalism reveals in our modern global economic system, and it became a threat to society.

## 5.5. A Critique of Money Power

Economic Capitalism outsources the power of Money which is seen throughout the global economic policy in the present context. The usage of money[354] was already introduced in the Roman Empire. In other words, money power becomes a big issue in those days because there is big discrimination among the citizens of Rome in terms of payment and salary. In order to clarify this, in 301 C.E. for example,

---

352 Tamas Szentes, *The Transformation of the World Economy: New Directions and New Interests* (London: Zed Books, 1988), 90.

353 Indukuri John Mohan Razu, *Global Capitalism as Hydra* (Delhi: ISPCK, 2006), 17.

354 Three different coins was in common use in ancient Rome:
*1) as* (pl.: *asses*), a bronze coin.
*2) sestertius* (pl.: *sestertii*; English "sesterce"), a silver coin.
*3) Denarius* (pl.: *denarii*), a silver coin.
Before the Second Punic War (218-201 B.C.E.):
2 ½ *assess* = 1 *sestertius*
10 *assess* = 1 *denarius*
4 *sestertii* = 1 *denarius*
After the Second Punic War:
4 *assess* = 1 *sestertius*
16 *assess* = 1 *denarius*
4 *sestertii* = 1 *denarius*
Another, smaller bronze coin, the *quadrans*, was worth about one-quarter of an *as*. (See Shelton, *As the Romans Did-A Source Book in Roman Social History*, 452).

sewer cleaners were paid 25 *denarii* a day, and carpenters and bakers were paid 60 *denarii* a day. Pork cost 12 *denarii* a pound. Thus, a sewer cleaner had to work a full day, a carpenter or baker a half-day, in order to earn the money to purchase two pounds of pork. Today, even workers at minimum wage can purchase the same amount of pork after about one hour of work. A very small number of people were enormously wealthy, while the vast majority could afford only basic necessities. At the time of Caesar (about 50 B.C.E.), for example, a senator had a property value of at least 800,000 sesterces (most had considerably more), while a rank-and-file soldier was paid 900 sesterces a year, and a labourer earned about 1000 sesterces, collected an income of 400,000 sesterces from another piece of property, and bequeathed almost 2,000,000 sesterces to support 100 of his freedmen, a soldier was paid 1200 sesterces a year. About 180 C.E., in the Roman province of Numidia (North Africa), 5 percent interest on 1,300,000 sesterces could support 600 children.[355] Not only is Rome down to the late fourth century a state without a coinage, in addition, no evidence that any use was made of the coinage of other states. The archaeological record of the city of Rome is devoid of coin finds earlier than the third century.[356]

Commercial Babylon (Rome), with its worship of money and power, will promote and push unrestrained luxury, sensuality and pleasure design to develop an all-consuming power over the masses via their uncontrolled lust pattern. Rome will promote the philosophy that happiness; significance, security, and fulfilment are attained by the abundance of the things people possess, in travel and

355 Shelton, *As the Romans Did-A Source Book in Roman Social History*, 452.

356 Michael H. Crawford, *Coinage and Money under the Roman Republic, Italy and the Mediterranean* (Los Angeles: University of California Press, 1985), 17. To consider first the invention of coinage, Pliny (claiming to follow Timaeus) attributed bronze coinage to Servius Tullius, while Varro thought that Servius Tullius produced silver coinage. An alternative tradition, starting from the similarity between Numa and nummus, attributed coinage to Numa Pompilius, the second king of Rome. A third tradition took the invention of coinage back to Saturn.

luxury, in comfort and pleasure.[357] In short, they are divided into two big groups-the rich and the poor. According to Warren Carter, "70-90% of the population did not have enough money to survive."[358] As being an oppressed group, it is, indeed, difficult to survive without the help of financial support.

From the light of Roman money power, the thread of money power and its impact had the same principle that still emerged in our present context. Marcos Arruda observes that Money had hypertrophied. The instrument that symbolised the real wealth created by humankind has itself been transformed, virtually, into real wealth. Like the Anti-Christ, who presents himself as the real Christ but is just hollow pretense, today's globalised capitalism has made a force of money. It is no longer represents real wealth, and this may be a fatal disease for global capitalism.[359] The state theory[360] studies money in relation to authority, rather than explaining the advent of money as a marker phenomenon.[361] In our present context, looking at the dimension of human life and activities, money becomes one of the most powerful machines and money became the most important element for holding power. The scenario of the Roman unjust economic system and money power could be seen in our context.[362]

---

357 J. Hampton Keathley III, *Studies in Revelation: Christ's Victory over the forces of Darkness*, (Biblical Studies Press, 2013). Cited 16 April 2017. Online: https://bible.org /seriespage/25-destruction-commercial-babylon-rev.

358 Carter, *Matthew and Empire,* 18.

359 Marcos Arruda, "Neo-liberal Financial Globalisation: Capitalism A Grave Illness," *Echoes* (15/1999), 20.

360 In the state theory, money is defined as a standard of value, suggesting that the source of monetary value lies in its support by a sovereign authority.

361 Georgios Papadopoulos, "Between Rules and Power: Money as an Institution Sanctioned by Political" *JEI* Vol. 43 No. 4 (December 2009), 951-969.

362 For example, In the Telangana State Election in 2018, as per election commission guidelines, each candidate can spend a maximum of Rs 28 lakh on his or her campaign, but according to political circles, for expenditure in these constituencies, the sky is the limit. Whatever the Election Commission guidelines say, in general, the average expenditure is around Rs 10 crore for each candidate. But in these constituencies, the expenditure may reach Rs 20 crore and above. Not only in the state of Telangana, but all the states in India, the most candidates also crossed the guidelines made by the Election Commission

There is no doubt that the excessive exercise of money power creates a lot of problems and injustice as the early centuries of the Roman Empire clearly portrayed and is still relevant in our present context. Money power devalued humanity and dehumanization is against the nature of God to His created human beings.

## 5.6. Babylonialism Today

Here, the term Babylonialism is used as a derogatory term in a metaphoric language to describe and reflect the unjust economic political activities of Rome. Babylon symbolized Rome in Revelation and it serve as an allusion to the Roman Empire, and Rome is the centre of oppressive imperialism that dominate the peasants, farmers and the lower class people. Thus, the researcher here used the term Babylonialism as a metaphor to address the unjust social and economic issues that the society faced today. This research described the issues and the real picture of the economic capitalism in the Roman Empire and also the parallelism in the present context of today. While discussing the image of the ancient Roman-Babylonialism in today's context, some important parallelism of Babylonialism in our context can be pointed out as follows.

### *Money Worship-Economic Crime against God*

The previous research of the critique of Roman economic policy clearly portrays the love of money among the ruling elites, further, the list of cargoes and the merchant's trade also portrays the excessive

---

of India in their campaign expenses due to the affirmation of money power. (See *Deccan Chronicle*, 21 Nov. 2018. n.p. [Cited 22 Nov. 2018]. Online: https://www.deccanchronicle.com/nation/current-affairs/211118/telangana-assembly-elections-money-power-in-play-in-20-seats.html.)

In one of the biggest political controversies ahead of Telangana Assembly Elections 2018, AIMIM chief Asaduddin Owaisi on Monday claimed that the Congress party tried to bribe him to cancel his public rally in Nirmal Assembly constituency in Adilabad district of the state. In a sensational charge, Owaisi on 19 Nov. (Monday) evening alleged that a Congress candidate offered him Rs 25 lakh to abstain from campaigning. (See *TimesNow*, 20th Nov. 2018. n.p. [Cited 22 Nov 2018]. Online: https://www.timesnownews.com/videos/shows/news/is-congress-using-money-power-for-mandate-the-newshour-debate-20th-november/15648).

wealth of Rome and her love of money. The ideology of money favouritism had seen in the ruling elites of the Roman Empire. Their excessive wealth portrays the huge amount of money and utilising money power and makes themselves blind to help the oppressed and marginalized. Rather, they urged a heavy burden of taxes, introducing economic injustice and social oppression upon the poor, subaltern and peasant/farmers.

In Revelation 13:17 "And lest anyone could buy or sell except the one having the mark, the name of the beast,"- here, the identifying mark (χαραγμα) was tantamount to a commercial license, those without it could neither buy nor sell,[363] citizens who do not bear the mark of the beast are not prevented from entering the markets, they are not able to buy their goods or sell them the necessities of life. David Aune also remarks that the inability to buy and sell apparently refers to the interdiction of basic and essential economic activity.[364] The close relationship between emperor worship and money worship is seen here.[365] In other words, those cannot buy or sell means that they should please the emperor (Emperor worship) if they want to buy and sell, because money (coins) was controlled by the emperor and the people were compelled to worship the emperor as God which is similar to money worship as the power of money was at the hand of the emperor. Even the emperor's image was stamped in the coins that show the authority of the emperor in commercial trade. Due to the economic exploitation and oppression, the people are pushed to worship emperor (so that they can buy and sell) which is parallel to the worshipping of money.[366] It is not surprising that the pursuit of

363 Ashcraft Morris, "Revelation" *BBC* Edited by Clifton J. Allen (Nashville: Broadman Press, 1972), 316. It takes but little imagination to grasp the seriousness of this economic boycott in the hands of a zealous and ambitious religious establishment.

364 Aune, *Revelation 6-16 WBC,* 768.

365 In the reign of Decius (Roman Emperor 249-51 C.E.) any man who did not possess the certificate of sacrifice to Caesar could not pursue ordinary trades but faced imprisonment, death or banishment. (See J. Massyngberde Ford, "*Revelation*" - *The Anchor Bible*. New York: Doubleday, 1975. 215).

366 In other NT writings, Apostle Paul clearly mentions the synonyms of this love of money. In 1 Tim 6:10, Paul use the word *φιλαργυρία,* which

wealth leads to ruin and destruction, for (gar) the love of money lies at the root of all kinds of evils (cf. 1 Tim 6:10).

### *Imperial Cult-Worship of Authorities for Self-Interest*

Critically examining the object of John's attack in Revelation, it is not only the Roman Empire, in and of itself. The object of John's attack is the worship of the emperor and empire which is equal to idolatry. Certainly, he believes that idolatry leads to injustice, exploitation, and abuse and that these things will be punished. But, the root of them all is idolatry.[367] The worshippers were given an elevated status and their outward faithfulness brought them prestige and power of the emperor and the other local deities.[368] The emperor cult never

---

represents the desire on the part of *οἱ βουλομενοι πλουτεων'* statement like this were well known in both Jewish and non-Jewish works. The closest is the words of Diogenes of Sinope: "The love of money is the mother city of all evil." *φιλαργυρία* (love of money) is what characterizes one who places his or her heart on possessing money, so violating the first commandment of the Decalogue, the commandment to love God (cf. Matt 6:24 par Luke 16:13). Because this is an expression of sinful self-love in opposition to love of God (cf. "lovers of self" and "lovers of money" in 2 Tim 3:2-4, a list concluding with the contrast "lovers of pleasure rather than lovers of God", cf. also Jas 4:4; 1 Jn 2:15), it also violates the inherently related second great commandment (Matt 22:39) to love one's neighbour. The result of those who had fallen in love with wealth, their undoing is described in two ways: First, they have left "faith." They have let go of commitment to the content of the Christian faith. Lust for wealth is thus depicted as a force that binds them and causes them to veer off course. Second, Paul uses the graphic language of an implement (they pierce themselves-*περιπειρω*) to describe the way in which these people cruelly harm themselves in pursuing the dream of wealth. (See George W. Knight III, *The Pastoral Epistle 1 Timothy: NIGTC.* Grand Rapids: Eerdmans Publishing, 1992. 257; Philip H. Towner, *The Letters to Timothy and Titus: NICNT.* Grand Rapids: Eerdmans, 2006. 403-404).

367 Christopher Bryan, *Render to Caesar: Jesus The Early Church and the Roman Superpower* (Oxford: Oxford University Press, 2005), 107.

368 David Naystrom, "We have no King but Caesar: Roman Imperial Ideology and the Imperial cult" in *Jesus is Lord, Caesar is not* Edited by Scot McKnight and Joseph B. Monica (Illinois: IVP Academic, 2013), 45.

became a new religion as such, rather a supplementary glorification of the official religion which served the Roman state.[369]

The parallel issue of the imperial cult in the Roman Empire is seen in today's context like worshipping the leaders in the society and the government authorities. Favouritism becomes a big stumbling block on the way of implementing justice, to become a member of the good books in the authorities for the personal interest is a big issue in the field of politics which causes various social unjust practices in our society. In the Roman Empire, the practice of Emperor Worship *vis-a-vis* favouritism of emperor compels the people to worship their earthly kings/authorities rather than anything in their life.

### *Misuse of Power and Authority*

This research proves that the prevailing conjunction of denying justice and misuse of power and authority in the Roman Empire; the top leaders, the ruling elites are being corrupted by oppressing and exploiting the peasants in the land. Bauckham investigates that religious corruption is offered in the cup whose golden exterior symbolizes the attraction of Rome's wealth and splendor. From John's Jewish Christian perspective, the political religion of Rome was the worst kind of false religion. John again felt that Rome's economic exploitation and the corrupting influence of her state religion go hand in hand.[370] Similarly, the same scenario in today's context-corruption[371] becomes one of the most common problems

369 Helmut Koester, *Introduction to the New Testament Vol. 1* (Philadelphia: Fortress Press, 1982), 370.

370 Bauckham, *The Climax of Prophecy*, 348-9.

371 M. A. Shewan and Udai Veer classify corruption into three parts: *Pretty corruption*, which means practicing on a smaller scale, defined as the use of public office for private benefit in the course of delivering a public service. Grand corruption, the most dangerous and convert type of corruption. Instances where policymaking, its design, and implementation are compromised by corrupt practices. Found where public officers in high positions (such as councillors), in the process of making decisions of significant economic value, routinely demand bribes or kickbacks for ensuring that tenders or contracts are awarded to specific contractors. Occurs financial, political and administrative centres of power. *Political Corruption* is the use of legislated powers by government officials for illegitimate private

in our society, a menace and also a burning issue today. It is the abuse of entrusted power for private gain[372] as we see the same misuse of power and authority in the Roman emperor. Ramsay argues that a key factor in Rome's fall was the steady loss of focus and control over government as its aims were thwarted for private gain by high-ranking bureaucrats and military leaders.[373] Thus, the misuse of power and authority in the realm of socio-religious political and economic causes the fall and decline of Rome. Likewise, corruption becomes a big stumbling block in just society.

In the present context in India, corruption linked with power that money and muscle power and other unfair means badly affected the morality of the people as we see the same scenario in the ruling elites of the Roman Empire. The ruling elites deeply involved in the misuse of power and authority that affects the whole society and is the major factor that God's judgment upon Rome. As likewise, Corruption is now recognized to be one of the world's greatest challenges. It is a major hindrance to sustainable development, with a disproportionate impact on poor communities and is corrosive on the very fabric of society.

## *The Problem of Debt*

The Roman wealth and power were mainly depended on land and consumed 65% of its production. Paying taxes was compulsory and not to pay taxes was regarded as a rebellion because it refused recognition of Rome's sovereignty over land, sea, labour, and production.[374] With regards to this, Money lending and loan system

gain. Misuse of government power for other purposes. (See M. A. Shewan and Udai Veer eds. *Corruption, Money Laundering and Law Part-1* New Delhi: Mittal Publications, 2011, 27).

372 "What is Corruption?" n.p. [Cited 26 Nov. 2018]. Online: https://www.transparency.org /what-is-corruption

373 Ramsay MacMullen, *Corruption and Decline of Rome* (Revised. Yale: Yale University Press, 1988). n.p. [Cited 26 Nov. 2018]. Online: https://books.google.co.in/books/yup? vid=ISBN9780300047998&redir_esc=y.

374 Carter, *The Roman Empire and the New Testament*, 3. The wealthy families of ruling elites built up large landed estates (by foreclosing in indebted peasant families' land. With their surplus wealth from booty and interest on loans they then bought large numbers of slaves captured by the legionaries in the

was also introduced in Roman Imperialism. Likewise, in our today's context, most people borrow a large sum of money from a bank or savings and loan institution; in ancient Rome, "bankers" were private individuals (mostly of ruling elites) with enough capital to make loans.[375] Due to the economic injustice, the peasant and farmers were not able to pay their debts and they entered into the slavery of debt. The level of taxation was much higher than other contemporaries' societies; they had to pay many types of taxes.[376] This causes a serious problem among the peasants (common people). The suffering of the peasants and slaves in the Roman Empire is a symbol of the Roman colonial system. It has been estimated that from 80 B.C.E. about 1.5 million people, roughly half the peasant families of Roman Italy, were forced off their ancestral lands. Many went to new lands in Italy, many were sent to Roman colonies in other lands, such as Corinth, and many simply migrated to the city of Rome and other towns in Italy. It is estimated that between 45 and 8 B.C.E. more than 250,000 adult males from Italy, roughly one-fifth of the 1.2 million who had lived there, were displaced from the Italian countryside. In a complimentary flow, over the course of the first century B.C.E., more than two million peasants from conquered provinces such as Judea were taken as slaves to Italy. By the end of the first century B.C.E., slaves amounted to about 35 to 40 percent of the total estimated population, the same percentage as the slaves in the southern United States in the nineteenth century.[377]

David Joy concludes that ordinary people lost their land and were forced to become bonded labourers under Roman rule and a rural

---

warlords' triumphant conquests and replaced the labour of the peasants, they had displaced. Slave labour was probably not any less expensive than free labour (peasants had fed themselves). But, the wealthy land-and slave-owners could control the labour of slaves far more than they could that of free labourers. (See Richard A. Horsley, *Jesus and the Powers: Conflicts, Covenant, and the Hope of the Poor* Minneapolis: Fortress Press, 2011, 27-28).

375 Shelton, *As the Romans Did-A Source Book in Roman Social History*, 136.

376 Joy, *Mark and Its Subalterns*, 80.

377 Keith Hopkins, *Conquerors and Slaves, Sociological Studies in Roman History* 1 (Cambridge: Cambridge University Press, 1978), 7, 67, 69.

economy became a slave-based one.[378] The present Indian context also struggles the problem of debt especially among the farmers; the economic injustice between the *zamindar* and the farmers creates a big gap and led to the suicide of farmers across the country.

## *Economic Justice/Capitalism*

Bauckham affirms that the inter-relatedness of economic exploitation and religion in the Roman economy by saying Rome's economic exploitation and the corrupting influence of her state religion go hand in hand.[379] Similarly, the homogenization of the world economy and globalisation of the western culture has been adversely affecting the communal harmony in the multi-cultural, multi-religious context like India. The fundamentalism that is associated with religious fanaticism has been undermining the values of the secularism and democracy.[380]

The global economy has witnessed mass scale production of food, clothing, transport, shelter etc. However, according to available data, millions of the world population suffer from hunger, lack of shelter, unemployment etc. In relation to this, the report of UNESCO (2015)[381] indicates the gross injustice done to the people in the global economy, many people face retrenchment or failure in their economic life. Many face discriminations in jobs, education and

378 Joy, *Mark and Its Subalterns,* 80.

379 Bauckham, *The Bible in Politics,* 91.

380 B. S. Shashikala, *The Portrayal of 'Rome' in the Book of Revelation: A Search for a Liberative Paradigm for the Subaltern Communities* (MTh Thesis, Senate of Serampore College, 2013), 99.

381 Marshal Fernando, "Religions and Economics Justice" in *Dialogue* New Series Vol. XLII & XLIII (2015-16): 3-5. According to the report: 58 million children are out of school; 100 million people are unable to read or write globally. State of the food insecurity in the world reported in FAO report 2015 states the following: 715 million people are in the world do not have enough food to lead a healthily active life. This is about 1 in 9 people on earth. The vast majority of these people live in developing countries where 12.9 percent of the population is undernourished. Poor nutrition causes nearly 45% of deaths in children under 5 years (3.1 million children each year). (See also n.p. [Cited 27 November 2018]. Online: http://unesdoc.unesco.org/images/0025/002503/250392e.pdf).

economic opportunities which are the result of economic injustice, so also called economic capitalism.

## 5.7. Conclusion

To conclude, in the economic capitalism, the main focus is on the fundamental human issues of survival: poverty, unemployment, discrimination, gender inequality and exploitation, oppression and marginalized, subaltern and dominance that are giving less attention towards criticising economic justice. The above discussion proved that economic injustice is the primary concern of human issues of survival. Therefore, from this point of view, economic exploitation becomes a serious crime against God. As Wesley Ariarajah opines that the biblical view of the economy could also be cast in this mode of thinking, 'Humans are not at the service of the economy, but the economy should be at the service of human beings' (cf. Mark 2:27).[382] The biblical view of the economy should be people-centred unless the practice of economic injustice/economic capitalism in society fails to serve its purpose.

382 S. Wesley Ariarajah, "Greed and Acquisitive attitude for wealth create an unjust society some Christian Perspective" *Dialogue* (NS) Vol. XLII-XLIII (2015-2016), 201-217.

Chapter 6

# General Conclusion

## 6.1. Introduction

This chapter provides a conclusion to the research as a whole, including the implications of the research and limitations as well as suggestions for further research. This research mainly focuses on the critique of economic capitalism in the Roman Empire from the socio-rhetorical reading. While criticising the economic issues in Revelation 18, the research focuses not only of the economic, but also the socio-political dimensions that shaped the Roman Economy. Reading the book of Revelation from the apocalyptic eye and studying from the lens of socio-rhetorical approach gives us an insight and deeper understanding of the milieu of the context of Revelation vis-à-vis unjust Roman economy. The research found out that the unjust economic structures of ancient Rome have the same dilemma in our present context which must be addressed.

## 6.2. General Summary

Chapter one, Chapter 2, gives out the general Introduction of the Research work. *Background and Context of the Book of Revelation* gives us information about a unique genre of Revelation that helps us to understand the book. The study also deals with the historical interpretation of Revelation which paved a way for the canonicity of the book. The apocalyptic genre of the book also helps us to perceive the meaning and background of the book which plays a crucial role in interpreting the book.

Chapter three, *The Identity of Babylon and Economic Issues in Revelation 18* helps us to understand the economic issues and the hidden agenda of the book. The quest of the identity of Babylon gives a new insight into the biblical understanding of the apocalyptic genre as well as prophetical usage. The various issues of economic in Revelation 18 give the socio-political and economic milieu of the Roman Empire and remind us that the economic crime is a big issue in the sight of God that occurs the reign of God upon Rome.

Chapter four, *Final Judgment upon the Unjust Economic Wealth of Rome: A Rhetorical Reading of Revelation 18*, this exegetical study paved the way for a creative discussion on the economic issues in Revelation 18. The rhetorical reading helps us to understand the socio-political and economic situation of Rome, the luxurious consumption and the arrogance of Rome which are clearly portrayed in this exegetical study. This study affirmed that Rome has benefited through the merchants, the kings of the earth and the sailors/shipmasters at the expense of many suffering people. Rome was judged principally as the practice of unjust economic wealth by exploiting the poor, the peasants and the oppressed.

Chapter five, *A Critique of Economic Capitalism in Roman Imperialism: It's Implication for Today's Context* analyses economic capitalism that can create a serious problem within the society at large. The study discovers that the allies of capitalism like money worship, corruption, problems of debt and economic injustice in the society seriously affect individual morality as well as the larger community in the society. The negative images of Babylonialism of ancient Rome are also a threat to our modern context.

## 6.3. Issues and Findings that Emerged from the Research

The research discloses that the economic issues in Revelation 18 have a serious crime against God, and, this study produces important issues that have to be addressed in our modern context.

i) The research proves that Revelation becomes one of the fiercest attacks on Rome and also is one of the most effective elements of political resistance literature from the period of the early Roman Empire. Stephen D. Moore also affirms that Revelation would appear to be an anti-imperial(istic) text that, in effect announces the transfer of worldwide *imperium* from the Roman Emperor to the heavenly emperor and his Son and co-regent, the 'King of kings, and Lord of lords' (19:16). Thus, Revelation merely re-inscribes, rather than effectively resists, Roman imperial ideology.[383]

ii) In the light of the critical study of the mourners of Rome in 18:3, the merchants became rich from the power of Rome's luxury which depends on the desire of Rome for luxury. Greed is the root of the matter behind this luxurious wealth, and it is one of the most frequently condemned elements in the New Testament. The long list of Rome's luxurious items also focused on the greed of the elites. Greed is the very same soulsickness in our culture that Revelation depicts in Rome and its allies-the lust for prosperity, wealth and luxury.

iii) The research ascertains that economic crime against God is one of the serious crimes in the Bible. Because economic crime collaborates with various negative companions as corruption, money power, unjust economic issues. As economics founded on the basic needs of humanity that God's creative nature was rooted in it, applying economic capitalism to annihilate just society could become a sin against God. As Ben Witherington III affirmed that Sin is not just a personal and private matter. It is woven into the very fabric of the fallen world and all its institution, be they political, economic, or religious.[384] The mighty Rome had to be rolled down from the top of arrogance and luxurious

383 Stephen D. Moore, 'The Revelation to John' in *A Postcolonial Commentary on the New Testament Writings* Edited by Fernando F. Segovia and R. S. Sugirtharajah (London: T&T Clark, 2007), 436-454.

384 Witherington III, *Jesus and Money*, 138.

economic wealth as she commits a crime against God through economic capitalism.

iv) This research of Economic Capitalism also reminds us that the strength and authority of Money power which is still a problem in our present context. If the Roman coins in the right hand, automatically power and authority would come up in the left hand, the same dilemma is found in today's context. The power and authority are in the hands of the rich and ruling class people, and power allied with favouritism that creates a gap between the just and unjust in the society. Monetary imperialism (also called money power vis-à-vis purchasing power) is a principal aspect of economic subjugation and it becomes a serious problem in our context.

v) From the perspective of the economic theme in Revelation 18, it is hard to avoid seeing a modern parallel in the economic relations with the ancient economy of Rome. Taking measure from our modern context, despite the difference of the context, the luxurious lives of the people have equally absurd forms of extravagant consumption. The collaboration between political powers and business leaders in Rome has the same image in our context. Even though Bauckham observes that the way in which Rome fed her own luxurious tastes by plundering and taxing her Empire is not paralleled in our post-colonial world, and this must warn us against any simplistic transference of judgment from the one case to the other.[385] But, in today's context, much had to be suggested that worship of material prosperity is equal to the emperor worship and worship of the idol in the ancient Roman world. The chief mourners of the fallen Rome may be the multinational companies, the advertising industry, and perhaps the arms trade. Thus, everyone should be aware of the hermeneutical trap that the author of Revelation laid for us beforehand.

---

385 Bauckham, *The Bible in Politics*, 102.

vi) The research provides a new lens of biblical hermeneutics. The unique apocalyptic genre of Revelation easily leads us into the trap of misinterpretation of the text. The rhetorical reading along with postcolonial lens of the text gives us new insight and also a deeper and true understanding of the message of the apocalypse. The rhetorical strategy creates a new symbolic universe that enables the readers to enter the new world and alienate themselves from the Roman power, and this paved a way for constructing a new social reality, a world of future possibility in the midst of oppression where God is the supreme sovereign. The research also found out that the apocalypse as resistance literature against Roman imperialism.

vii) From the light of the research, it is true that understanding the book of Revelation as apocalyptic literature encouraged us to understand the real-world situations, depicted in cosmic terms, that it reflects and addresses.[386] It also encourages us not to take the symbolism literally rather it appeals to the imagination to address the most profound realities that God's people can experience for or hope for. Hope in apocalyptic literature plays a crucial role in reading the text within the text.

viii) The economic discrepancies of Rome are a threat to our present context. The economic issues in Revelation 18 are a perfect example of today's context. The list of the cargoes in 18:13 shows that it mostly centred around the luxurious lifestyle of the rich class people. The capitalistic mentality of the ruling elites also portrays the corrupted minds of the rich-ruling elites. The present society must have a lesson to learn from the unjust economic discrepancies of Rome as our society is struggling with unjust socio-political dimensions.

## 6.4. Limitations and Suggestions

The research had limitations in terms of hermeneutics and postcolonial view. The book of Revelation itself has a different style

386 Gorman, *Reading Revelation Responsibly*, 21.

and genre which is somehow difficult to grasp with the context, the misuse of the term 'apocalypse' in a theological concept to this very day in many scholar's publications, the research is limited to go deeper into that field. In fact, this research somehow gives a hint to put a new lens of viewing apocalypse from different angles. The research mainly focused on the economic issues in the book especially in Revelation 18, the theological concept and the detailed study of the OT prophetic interrelatedness is not much dealt with in the study. The biblical hermeneutics of socio-rhetorical reading also needs to improve by reflecting the present context. A deeper study of apocalyptic literature also needs to be updated and more research could be done in this field. When comparing the unjust economic issues between the text and the modern context, the present economic juncture is lacking in the research due to the limited space, further study should be suggested.

Appendix-1

# The Seven Churches in Asia Minor Addressee of the Book of Revelation

## *The Patmos Background*

Patmos harbour is situated some 40 miles from the mouth of the Maeander (Büyük Menderes), the nearest point of the Asian mainland, and about 65 miles from the site of Ephesus. The island is 60km gap off the modern Turkish coast. The island is 8 miles long and 5 wide, and according to Pliny, it measures 30 Roman miles in circumference. The modern town of Patmos clusters around the eleventh-century monastery on the summit of Ăyios Elias, the 800-foot eminence above, which dominates the southern half of the island.

## *The Seven Churches in Asia Minor*

1. *Ephesus*: The original Greek settlement, perhaps dating from about 1100 B.C.E. was established in territory occupied by indigenous peoples, Carians, and Leleges, and the tribal structure which persisted indicates a continuing mixture of race and culture in the citizen body. The earliest site was on the northern slope of Pion. The sea must then have come close to the hill. The ancient temple of the great goddess identified with Artemis

stood less than a mile outside the walls. Ephesus reached the height of its wealth and influence in the Hellenistic and Roman periods. When Rome assumed power in 133 B.C.E. under the terms of the bequest of Attalus III, this wealthy seaport was open to exploitation by ruthless officials. The commercial prosperity of Ephesus was under the potential threat of the irrevocable silting of the harbor. Strabo was aware of the danger and records that the engineers of Attalus Philadelphus had already worsened the situation by a faulty attempt to deepen the entrance. At the present-day Ephesus has all the appearance of an inland city. The most impressive view of modern Ephesus is from the western side of Mount Pion, either from the upper seats of the great theatre or from a point a little higher.

2. *Smyrna*: Smyrna was founded as a Greek colony more than a thousand years before Christ, but that ancient Aeolian Smyrna was soon captured by Ionian Greeks and made into an Ionian colony. Ionian Smyrna was a great city, whose armies contended on even terms against the power of Lydia. This Asiatic Smyrna between about 600-290 B.C.E. was a loose aggregate of villagers living in various settlements scattered over the plain and the surrounding hills. It possessed no sovereign power or self-governing institutions, and it has left no trace on history. Smyrna had a close relationship with Rome, as early as 195 B.C.E., when Antiochus was still at the height of his power; Smyrna built a temple and instituted worship of Rome. Today Smyrna is the modern Turkish city of Izmir, situated at the head of the Gulf of Izmir and an important port.
3. *Pergamum*: Pergamum, the modern Turkish town of Bergama. The citadel of Pergamum was built on a cone shaped hill rising 300m above the surrounding valley. It was here that a famous library containing 200,000 scrolls was established in the reign of Eumenes II (197-159 B.C.E.). In 133 B.C.E. Rome made the city the capital in its new province of Asia. The citadel of Pergamum was the site of the celebrated altar of Zeus, some have identified this with "Satan's throne" mentioned by John in Revelation 2:13.

4. *Thyatira*: Thyatira, the modern Turkish town of Akhisar, was famous in antiquity as a centre for the manufacture of purple cloth. Lydia, a dealer in purple cloth whom Paul met at Philippi, was from Thyatira. Another important industry was the manufacture of burnished bronze, alluded to in Revelation 2:18. Other trades are known to have flourished in the town. Membership of trade guilds would have involved an attendance at guild meetings, with their paganism and accompanying immorality.
5. *Sardis*: Sardis, the modern Turkish village of Sart, was the capital of the ancient kingdom of Lydia. During the reign of the Lydian king Gyges (c. 680-644 B.C.E.) gold was discovered in the Pactolus River, which runs through Sardis, and Lydia introduce the world's first coinage in gold, silver and electrum. In the last couple of centuries B.C.E. there was considerable Jewish settlement in the area. The Synagogue at Sardis is the largest ancient synagogue known.
6. *Philadelphia*: Philadelphia, the modern Turkish town of Alasehir was established as a frontier fort of Pergamum in 189 B.C.E. The name means "brotherly love" commemorating the love of Eumenes II (197-159 B.C.E.) of Pergamum for his younger brother, Attalus. A ruined Byzantine church is the only witness to a Christian past. In relation to Rome, Philadelphia shared in the bounty of the emperor Tiberius and took part with the other cities in erecting in Rome a monument commemorating their gratitude. It also founded a cult of Germanicus, the adopted son and heir of Tiberius (according to the will of Augustus), who was in Asia at that time. Because of this connection, the city's prosperity was seriously impaired, and no coins were struck by it throughout the reign of Tiberius.
7. *Laodicea*: Laodicea located near the village of Goncah, north of Denizli.The city was named by the Seleucid king Antiochus II after his wife Laodice. Between Laodicea and the "Gate of Phrygia" lay a famous temple, the home of the Phrygian god Men Karou, the Carian Men. This was the original god of the valley. His temple was the centre of the society and administration, intercourse and trade, as well as of religion. A market was held

under the protection of his sacred name, beside or in his own precinct, at which the people of the valley met and traded with strangers from a distance, and this market continued to meet weekly in the same place until about fifty years ago, when it was moved two or three north to the new village called Serai-Keui (Sarayköy). The Laodicean church is the only one which is absolutely and wholly condemned. Not even a faithful remnant is left, such as even in Sardis, the dead church kept itself pure and white. No exception is allowed in Laodicea.

## *References*

*Hemer, Colin J. The Letters to the Seven Churches of Asia in their Local Setting. Grand Rapids: Eerdmans Publishing, 1989.*

*Johnson, Richard ed., The IVP Concise Atlas of Bible History. Illinois: IVP Academic, 2013.*

*Ramsay, W. M. The Letters to the Seven Churches. Updated Edition; USA: Hendrickson Publishers, 1994.*

# Bibliography


## 1. Primary Sources

Rienecker, Fritz. *A Linguistic Key to the Greek New Testament.* Grand Rapids: Zondervan Publishing House, 1980.

*The Greek New Testament.* Fourth Revised Edition. Stuttgart: United Bible Societies, 2005.

*The Holy Bible, New Revised Standard Version.* Nashville: Catholic Bible Press, 1989.

## 2. Dictionaries/Lexicon/Encyclopaedia

Arnold, Bill T. "Revelation, Book of." Pages 376-380 in *The New Interpreters Dictionary of the Bible.* Edited by Katharine Doob Sakenfeld. Nashville: Abingdon Press, 2006.

Blickenstaf, Marainne. "Pax Romana." Pages 421-422 in vol. 4 of *New Interpreters Dictionary of the Bible.* Edited by Katharine Doob Sakenfeld. Nashville: Abingdon Press, 2006.

Bikes, Gerald M. "Money, Coins." Pages 130-137 in *New Interpreters' Dictionary of the Bible.* Edited by Katharine Doob Sakenfeld. Nashville: Abingdon Press, 2006.

Botta, Alejandro F. "Slaves, Slavery." Pages 1232-1233 in *The Eerdmans Dictionary of Early Judaism.* Edited by John J. Collins and Daniel C. Harlow. Grand Rapids: Eerdmans, 2010.

Collins, Adela Yarbro, "Revelation, Book of." Pages 694-695 in vol. 5 of *The Anchor Bible Dictionary.* Edited by David Noel Freedman. 5 Vols. New York: Doubleday, 1992.

Cirlot, J. E., *A Dictionary of Symbols*. New York: Routledge & Kegan, 1962.

Elwell, Walter A., *Baker's Evangelical Dictionary of Biblical Theology.* Grand Rapids: Baker Book House, 1996.

Evans, Craig A. and Stanley E. Porter. eds., *Dictionary of New Testament Background.* Illinois: InterVarsity Press, 2000.

Balz, Horst and Gerhard Schneider. *Exegetical Dictionary of the New Testament*, Vol. 2. Reprinted. Grand Rapids: Eerdmans, 2000.

Harill, J. Albert. "Slavery." Pages 299-308 in *New Interpreters' Dictionary of the Bible.* Edited by Katharine Doob Sakenfeld. Nashville: Abingdon Press, 2006.

Kepler, T. S. "Revelation, Book of." Page 850 in *Dictionary of the Bible*. Edited by James Hastings. Second Edition. Edinburg: T&T Clark, 1963.

Ladd, G. E. "Revelation, Book of," Pages 171-177 in *The International Standard Bible Encyclopaedia.* Edited by Geoffrey W. Bromiley. Vol. 4 Q-Z. Grand Rapids: Eerdmans Publishing Company, 1988.

Mackenzie, J. A. Ross. "Symbol." Pages 1003-1007 in *Harper's Bible Dictionary.* Edited by Paul . Achtemeier. San Francisco: Harpers & Row, 1985.

Murray, G. R. Beasley. "Revelation, Book of." Pages 1025-1038 in *Dictionary of the Later New Testament and Its Developments.* Edited by Ralph P. Martin and Peter H. Davids. England: InterVarsity Press, 1997.

Murray, G. R. Beasley, "Revelation, Book of." Pages 924-936 In *The IVP Dictionary of the New Testament.* Edited by Daniel G. Reid. England: InterVarsity Press, 2004.

Rust, Eric C. "Symbols." Page 865 in *Mercer Dictionary of the Bible.* Edited by Watson E. Mills. Georgia: Mercer University Press, 1990.

Spicq, Ceslas. *Theological Lexicon of the New Testament* Vol. 1. Translated by James D.Ernst. Masachusetts: Hendrickson, 1994.

Wainwright, A. W. "Revelation, Boof of." Page 393 In *Dictionary of Biblical Interpretation K-Z.* Edited by John H. Hayes. Nashville: Abingdon Press, 1999.

## 3. Commentaries


Allen, Cliften J. ed., *The Broadman Bible Commentary Volume 12-Revelation.* USA: Broadman Press, 1972.

Aune, David E., *Word Biblical Commentary-Revelation Volume 52.* Dallas, Texas: Word Books Publishers, 1997.

Boring, M. E., *Revelation-Interpretation.* Louisville: John Knox, 1989.

Beale, G. K., *The Book of Revelation: The New International Greek Testament Commentary.* Grand Rapids: Eerdmans, 2013.

______ *Revelation-A Shorter Commentary.* Grand Rapids: Eerdsman Publishing Company, 2015.

Charles, R. H., *A Critical and Exegetical Commentary on The Revelation of St. John – International Critical Commentary* vol. 2. Reprinted. Edinburgh: T&T Clark, 1959.

DeSilva, David A., *Perseverance in Gratitude: A Socio-Rhetorical Commentary on the Epistle to the Hebrews.* Grand Rapids: Eerdsmans, 2000.

Ford, J. Massyngberde. *Revelation-The Anchor Bible Commentary.* New York: Doubleday. 1975.

Gonzâlez, Catherine Gunsalus and Justol L. Gonzâlez. *Revelation* Louisville, Kentucky: John Knox Press, 1997.

Hagelberg, Dave. *The Revelation of Jesus Christ Chapters 12-22.* Delhi: ISPCK, 2013.

Knight III, George W., *The Pastoral Epistle (1 Timothy): The New International Greek Testament Commentary.* Grand Rapids: Eerdmans, 1992.

Kistemaker, Simon J., *New Testament Commentary-Exposition of the Book of Revelation.* Grand Rapids: Baker Books, 2001.

Morris, C. L. *The Revelation of St. John: An Introduction and Commentary.* London: Tyndale Press, 1969.

Mounce, Robert H., *The Book of Revelation: New International Commentary of New Testament.* Revised Edition. Grand Rapids: Eerdmans, 1998.

Mounce, Robert H. *The New International Commentary on the New Testament.* Cambridge: Eerdmans, 1977.

Roloff, Jurgen. *Revelation-A Continental Commentary.* Translated by John E. Alsup. Minneapolis: Fortress Press, 1993.

Rowland, Christopher. *Revelation.* London: Epworth, 1993.

Swete, Henry Barclay. *The Apocalypse of St. John: The Greek Text with Introduction Notes and Indices.* New York: Macmillan Company, 1906.

______ *The Apocalypse of St. John: The Greek Text with Introduction, Notes and Indices.* Grand Rapids: Eerdmans, 1951.

Sweet, John. *Revelation.* London: SCM Press, 1990.

Smalley, Stephen S., *The Revelation to John: A Commentary on the Greek Text of the Apocalypse.* Illinois: InterVarsity Press, 2005.

Segovia, Fernando F., and R. S. Sugirtharajah. Eds., *A Postcolonial Commentary on the New Testament Writings.* London: T&T Clark, 2007.

Thomas, Robert L., *Revelation 8-22: An Exegetical Commentary.* Chicago: Moody Publishers, 1995.

Towner, Philip H., *The Letters to Timothy and Titus: The New International Commentary on the New Testament.* Grand Rapids: Eerdmans, 2006.

Thomas, M. M., *The Revelation to John.* Tiruvalla: CSS Books, 2014.

Waller, E. H. M., *The Revelation of St. John the Divine with Introduction and Notes.* Madras: London SPCK, 1926.

Witherington III, Ben. *Revelation-The New Cambridge Bible Commentary.* UK: Cambridge University Press, 2003.

## 4. Monographs

Alfrod, Henry. *The Greek Testament.* London: Longmans, Green, 1903.

Arms, J. H. D. and E. C. Kopff. eds., *The Seaborne Commerce of Ancient Rome: Studies in Archaeology and History.* Rome: American Academy, 1980.

Alexander, Loveday. ed., *Images of Empire.* JSOTSS 122. Sheffield: Sheffield Academic Press, 1991.

Abir, A. Peter. *Conflict and Conquest: An Exegetico-Theological Study of Revelation 12, 7-12.* Bangalore: Asian Trading Corporation, 1998.

Aune, David. ed., *The Blackwell Companion to the New Testament.* London: Wiley Blackwell, 2010.

Badian, Ernest. *Roman Imperialism in the Late Republic.* Ithaca: Cornell University Press, 1968.

Boesak, A., *Comfort and Protest: The Apocalypse from a South African Perspective.* Philadelphia: Westminster, 1986.

Brunt, Peter. *Roman Imperial Themes.* Oxford: Claredon, 1990.

Bauckham, Richard. *The Bible in Politics-How to Read the Bible Politically.* Britain: SPCK, 1989.

______ *The Theology of The Book of Revelation.* New York: Cambridge University Press, 1993.

______ *The Climax of Prophecy: Studies on the Book of Revelation.* Edinburgh: T&T Clark, 1993.

Brook, Wes-Howard. and Anthony Gwyther. *Unveiling Empire-Reading Revelation Then and Now.* New York: Orbis Books, 2002.

Bhabha, Homi., *The Location of Culture.* London: Routledge, 2004.

Bryan, Christopher. *Render to Caesar: Jesus The Early Church and the Roman Superpower.* Oxford: Oxford University Press, 2005.

Barr, David L., *The Reality of Apocalypse: Rhetoric and Politics in the Book of Revelation.* Atlanta: Society of Biblical Literature, 2006.

Black, C. Clifton. and Duane F. Watson eds., *Studies in Rhetoric and Religion 8.* Waco: Baylor University Press, 2008.

Charlesworth, M. P., *The Roman Empire.* Reprinted. London: Oxford University Press, 1961.

Court, John M., *Myth and History in the Book of Revelation.* London: ISPCK, 1979.

Collins, A. Y., *Crisis and Catharsis: The Power of the Apocalypse.* Philadelphia: Westminster Press, 1984.

Clevenot, Michel. *Materialistic Approaches to the Bible.* Translated by William J. Nottingham. New York: Orbis Books, 1985.

Crawford, Michael H., *Coinage and Money Under the Roman Republic, Italy and the Mediterranean.* Los Angeles: University of California Press, 1985.

Couch, Mal. ed., *A Bible Handbook to Revelation.* Grand Rapids: Kregel Publications, 2001.

Carter, Warren. *Matthew and Empire: Initial Exploration*, Harrisburg: Trinity Press International, 2001.

______ *The Roman Empire and the New Testament-An Essential Guide.* Nashville: Abingdon Press, 2006.

______ *John and Empire-Initial Explorations.* New York: T&T Clark, 2008.

Dunn, James D. G., *Unity and Diversity in the New Testament.* London: SCM Press, 1977.

D'Souza, Albert. *Studies in Religious Imagination and Symbolism.* New Delhi: A Mittal Publication, 2005.

deSilva, David A., *Seeing things John's Way: The Rhetoric of the Book of Revelation.* Louisville: John Knox Press, 2009.

Eliade, Mircea. *Images and Symbols- Studies in Religious Symbolism.* New York: Search Book Edition, 1969.

Frank, T. ed., *An Economic Survey of Ancient Rome* vol. 5 Baltimore: John Hopkins Press, 1940.

Ford, J. Massyngberde. *Revelation- The Anchor Bible.* New York: Doubleday, 1975.

Friedman, Milton. *Capitalism and Freedom.* Chicago: The University of Chicago Press, 1982.

Fiorenza, Elisabeth Schussler. *The Book of Revelation: Justice and Judgement.* Philadelphia: Fortress Press, 1985.

Freed, Edwin D., *The New Testament: A Critical Introduction.* Second Edition. USA: Wadsworth Publishing Company, 1991.

______ *Revelation: Vision of a Just World.* Edinburgh: T&T Clark, 1993.

Friesen, Stenven J., *Imperial Cults and the Apocalypse of John: Reading Revelation in the Ruins.* New York: Oxford University Press, 2001.

Fiensy, D. A., *The Social History of Palestine in the Herodian Period. The Land is Mine.* New York: Edwin Mellen Press, 1991.

Giardina, Andrea. ed., *The Romans.* Chicago: University of Chicago Press, 1993.

Gorman, Michael J., *Reading Revelation Responsibly.* USA: Cascade Books, 2011.

Hopkins, Keith. *Conquerors and Slaves, Sociological Studies in Roman History 1.* Cambridge: Cambridge University Press, 1978.

Horsley, Richard A., *Jesus and the Spiral of Violence: Popular Jewish Resistance in Roman Palestine.* San Francisco: Harper and Row, 1987.

______ *Paul and Empire: Religion and Power in Roman Imperial Society.* Harrisburg: Trinity Press International, 1997.

______ *Sociology and Jesus Movement,* Second Edition. New York: The Continuum Publication,1999.

______ *Jesus and the Powers: Conflicts, Covenant, and the Hope of the Poor.* Minneapolis: Fortress Press, 2011.

Hagelberg, Dave. *The Revelation of Jesus Christ to the Seven Churches and to us Chapters 1-11.* Delhi: ISPCK, 2013.

Jones, A. H. M., *The Later Roman Empire 282-602* vol. 2. UK: Basil Blackwell, 1986.

Jones, Arthur. *Capitalism and Christians-Through Gospel Challenges in a Troubled World Economy.* New York: Paulist Press, 1992.

Joy, C. I. David., *Revelation- A Post-colonial Viewpoint.* Delhi: ISPCK, 2001.

______ *Mark and Its Subalterns.* London: Equinox, 2008.

Johnson, Luke Timothy. *The Writings of the New Testament: An Interpretation.* 3rd Edition. Minneapolis: Fortress, 2010.

Koch, Klaus. *The Rediscovery of Apocalyptic.* London: SCM Press, 1972.

Kautsky, John. *The Politics of Aristocratic Empires.* Chapel Hill: University of North Carolina Press, 1982.

Koester, Helmut. *Introduction to the New Testament* Vol. 1. Philadelphia: Fortress Press, 1982.

Kraybill, J. Nelson. *Imperial Cult and Commerce in John's Apocalypse,* Journal of Studies of New Testament Supplement 132. Sheffield: Sheffield Academic Press, 1996.

______ *Apocalypse and Allegiance: Worship, Politics and Devotion in the Book of Revelation.* Grand Rapids: Brazos Press, 2010.

Keathlwy III, J. Hampton. *Studies in Revelation: Christ's Victory over the forces of Darkness.* Biblical Studies Press, 2013.

Leeman, Wayne A., *Capitalism, Market Socialism and Central Planning.* Delhi: Khosla & Co., 1976.

Levick, Barbara. *The Government of Roman Empire.* London: Routledge, 2000.

McNamara, Martin. *Intertestamental Literature.* USA: Michael Glazier Inc., 1983.

Meeks, Wayne A., *The First Urban Christians: The Social World of the Apostle Paul.* London: Yale University Press, 1983.

MacMullen, Ramsay. *Corruption and Decline of Rome.* Revised. Yale: Yale University Press, 1988

Makhikani, Arjun. *From Global Capitalism to Economic Justice.* New York: The Apex Press, 1992.

Matthew, Sam P., *Temple-Criticism in Mark's Gospel.* Delhi: ISPCK, 1999.

Maier, Harry O., *Apocalypse Recalled- The Book of Revelation after Christendom.* Minneapolis: Fortress Press, 2002.

Mitchell, Margaret M. and Frances M. Young. eds., *Origin to Constantine.* Cambridge: Cambridge University Press, 2006.

Murphy, Frederick J., *Apocalypticism in the Bible and Its World.* Grand Rapids: Baker Academic, 2012.

McKnight, Scot. & Joseph B. Monica. *Jesus is Lord, Caesar is not.* Illinois: IVP Academic, 2013.

Nickelsburg, George W. E., *The Apocalyptic Construction for Reality in 1 Enoch.* Glasgow: Collins and Charlesworth: 1991.

Oppenheim, A. Leo. *Ancient Mesopotamia.* Revised Edition. Chicago: University of Chicago Press, 1977.

Olson, Alan M. ed., *Myth, Symbol and Reality.* London: University of Notre Dame Press, 1980.

Oakes, Peter. ed., *Rome in the Bible and the Early Church.* UK: Paternoster Press, 2002.

Parkins, Helen. eds., *Roman Urbanism: Beyond the Consumer City.* London: Routledge, 1997.

Park, Rohun. *The Bible and Critical Theory*, Vol. 4. Australia: Monarch University Press, 2008.

Ramsay, W. M., *The Letters to the Seven Churches of Asia.* London: Hodder & Stoughton, 1904.

Russell, D. S., *The Method and Message of Jewish Apocalyptic.* Reprinted. London: SCM Press, 1971.

Rostovtzeff, M., *The Social and Economic History of the Roman Empire*, 2 Vols. Second Edition. Oxford: Clarendon Press, 1979.

Roy, Ajit. *On Marxist Theory and Practice: From Stalin and Mao to Gorbachev and Deng.* Calcutta: The Marxist Review Publications, 1992.

Reimer, David J. *The Oracles against Babylon in Jeremiah 50-51: A Horror among the Nations.* San Francisco: Mellen Research University Press, 1993.

Robbins, Vernon K., *Exploring the Texture of Texts: A Guide to Socio-Rhetorical Interpretation.* Pennsylvania: Trinity Press International, 1996.

Rowlandson, J., *Women and Society in Greek and Roman Egypt.* Cambridge: Cambridge University Press, 1998.

Rossing, Barbara R., *The Choice of Between Two Cities-Whore, Bride and Empire in the Apocalypse.* USA: Trinity Press International, 1999.

Razu, Indukuri John Mohan. *Global Capitalism as Hydra.* Delhi: ISPCK, 2006.

Saggs, H. W. F., *The Greatness That was Babylon.* New York: Hawthorn Books Inc., 1962.

Stringfellow, William. *An Ethic for Christians and Other Aliens in a Strange Land.* Texas: Word Books, 1973.

Szentes, Tamas. *The Transformation of the World Economy-New Direction and New Interests.* Tokyo: Zed Books Ltd., 1988.

Sweezy, Paul M., *The Theory of Capitalist Development.* Indian Edition. New Delhi: KP Bagchi & Company, 1991.

Shelton, Jo-Ann. *As the Romans Did-A Source Book in Roman Social History.* Second Edition. Oxford: Oxford University Press, 1998.

Schneidel, Walter. *Slavery in the Roman Economy.* Stanford: Stanford University, 2010.

Shewan, M. A., and Udai Veer. eds. *Corruption, Money Laundering and Law Part-1.* New Delhi: Mittal Publications, 2011.

Scheidel, Walter. ed., *The Cambridge Companion to the Roman Economy.* Cambridge: Cambridge University Press, 2012.

Sea, Pyung Soo. *Luke's Jesus in the Roman Empire and the Emperor in the Gospel of Luke.* Oregon: Pickwick Publications, 2015.

Thiessen, Henry Clarence. *Introduction to the New Testament.* Fourth Edition. Grand Rapids: Eerdmans, 1948.

Walvoord, John F., *The Millennial Kingdom.* Findlay, Ohio: Dunham, 1939.

Wallerstein, Immanuel. *The Politics of World Economy.* London: Cambridge University Press, 1984.

Whittaker, C. R., *Land, City and Trade in the Roman Empire-* Collected Studies 408. Aldershot: Variorum, 1993.

Witherington III, Ben. *Jesus & Money.* Great Britain: SPCK, 2010.

## 5. Journal/Articles

Aune, D. E., "The Form and Functions of the Proclamations to the Seven Churches (Revelation 2-3)." *New Testament Studies* Vol. 36, (1990): 182-204.

Arruda, Marcos. "Neo-liberal Financial Globalisation: Capitalism 'A Grave Illness." *Echoes* (15/1999): 20.

Ariarajah, S. Wesley. "Greed and Acquisitive Attitude for Wealth Create an Unjust Society Some Christian Perspective." *Dialogue* (NS) Vols. XLII-XLIII (2015-2016): 201-217.

Bauckham, Richard. "Judgment in the Book of Revelation." *Ex Auditu*, 20 (2004), 1-24.

Biguzzi, G., "Is the Babylon of Revelation Rome or Jerusalem?" *Biblica* Vol. 87 No. 3 (2006): 371-386.

Benedict, James. "The Great Whore Cast Down: Revelation 17-18 and the Imagery of Roman Conquest." *Brethren Life and Thought*, 61 No. 1 (Spring 2016): 39-48.

Collins, J. J. "The Political Perspective of the Revelation to John." *Journal of Biblical Literature* 96 (1977): 241-256.

Carter, Warren. "Paying the Tax to Rome as Subversive Praxis: Matthew 17.24-27." *Journal of Studies of the New Testament 76* (1999): 3-31.

Callahan, Allen D., "Apocalypse as Critique of Political Economy: Some Notes on revelation 18." *Horizons in Biblical Theology* Vol. 21 (1999): 46-65.

Dyson, Stephen. "Native Revolts in the Roman Empire." *Historia 20* (1971): 239-74.

Finley, M. I., "Empire in the Greco Roman World." *Greece and Rome* Vol. 25, No. 1 (Apr 1978): 11-12.

Friesen, Steven J., "Poverty in Pauline Studies: Beyond the So-called New Consensus." *Journal of Studies of the New Testament* 26 (2004): 323-61.

______ "Satan's Throne, Imperial Cults and the Social Settings of Revelation." *Journal of Studies of the New Testament* 27.3 (2005): 351-373.

Fernando, Marshal "Religions and Economics Justice." *Dialogue* New Series Vol. XLII & XLIII (2015-16): 3-5.

Georgi, Dieter. "Who is the True Prophet?" *Harvard Theological Review* 79 (1986): 125.

Gregory, Peter F. "Its End Is Destruction: Babylon the Great in the Book of Revelation." *Concordia Theological Quarterly*, No. 73 (2 April 2009): 137-153.

Kallas, James "The Apocalypse – an Apocalyptic Book?" *Journal of Biblical Literature*, lxxxvi, (1967): 69-80.

Koester, Craig R. "Roman Slave Trade and the Critique of Babylon in Revelation 18." *The Catholic Biblical Quarterly* 70 (2008): 765-786.

Maier, Harry O., "Staging the Gaze: Early Christian Apocalypses and Narrative Self-Representation." *Harvard Theological Review* 90 (1997): 149-50.

Oden Jr. Robert A., "Taxation in Biblical Israel." *The Journal of Religious Ethics*, Vol. 12, No. 2 (1984): 162-181.

Oakman, Douglas E., "The Ancient Economy and St. John's Apocalypse." *Listening* 28 (1993): 200-214.

Perry, Peter S., "Critiquing the Excess of Empire: A Synkrisis of John of Patmos and Dio of Prusa." *Journal for the Study of the New Testament* 29.4 (2007): 473-496.

Park, Rohun. "Revelation for Sale: In Intercultural Reading of Revelation 18 From an East Asian Perspective." *The Bible and Critical Theory*, Vol. 4 No. 2 (2008): 25.1-25.10

Papadopoulos, Georgios. "Between Rules and Power: Money as an Institution Sanctioned by Political." *Journal of Economic Issue* Vol. 43 No. 4 (December 2009): 951-969.

Royalty, Robert M. Jr., "Don't touch this Book! Revelation 22:18-19 and the Rhetoric of Reading (in) the Apocalypse of John." *Biblical Interpretation-A Journal of Contemporary Approaches* Vol. XII, 3, (2004): 285.

Singer, J. David. "Inter-Nation Influence: A Formal Model." *American Political Science Review*, 57 (June 1963): 420.

Strand, Kenneth. "Some Modalities of Symbolic Usage in Revelation 18." *Andrews University Seminary Studies* (AUSS) 24 (1986): 37-46.

Smith, Christopher R. "The Structure of the Book of Revelation in light of Apocalyptic Literary Conventions." *Novum Testamentum* XXXVI, Fasc. (4 Oct., 1994): 380.

Slater, Thomas B., "On the Social Setting of the Revelation to John." *New Testament Studies* Vol. 44, (1998, 2 April): 232-256.

Temin, Peter. "A Market Economy in the Early Roman Empire." *The Journal of Roman Studies*, Vol. 91 (2001): 169-181.

## 6. Unpublished Thesis/Papers

Gummalolla, Soleman. "Postcolonial Interpretation of Apocalyptic Symbolism as a mode of Resistance in Revelation" DTh Thesis, Senate of Serampore College, 2016.

Shashikala, B. S. "The Portrayal of 'Rome' in the Book of Revelation: A Search for a Liberative Paradigm for the Subaltern Communities" MTh Thesis, Senate of Serampore College, 2013.

Samuel, Joseph. "Wealth and Possesion in the Gospel According to Luke: An early Christian Alternative to Roman Imperial Economy" MTh Thesis, Senate of Serampore College, 2010.

Wilson, J.C. "Babylon as Cipher for Rome and Dating of Early Jewish and Early Christian Documents." Unpublished Paper read at the 1994 Annual Meeting of the Society of Biblical Literature.

## 7. Websites and Blogs

*Deccan Chronicle*, 21 Nov. 2018. No Pages. Cited 22 Nov. 2018. Online: https://www.deccanchronicle.com/nation/current-affairs/211118/telangana-assembly-elections-money-power-in-play-in-20-seats.html.

Finger, Reta Halteman. "Conflict and Crisis in Asia Minor." No Pages. Cited 13 July 2018. Online: https://eewc.com/conflict-crisis-asia-minor-revelation-2-3/.

Mark, Joshua J., "Asia Minor." *Ancient History Encyclopaedia*. Online Edition. Published on 4th May, 2018. Cited 13 July 2018. Online: https://www.ancient.eu/Asia_Minor/].

"Telangana 2018 Assembly Election." *TimesNow*, 20th Nov. 2018. No Pages. Cited 22 Nov. 2018. Online: https://www.timesnownews.com/videos/shows/news/is-congress-using-money-power-for-mandate-the-newshour-debate-20th-november/15648).

UNESCO 2015 Report. No Pages. Cited 27 Nov. 2018. Online: http://unesdoc.unesco.org/images/0025/002503/250392e.pdf.

"What is Corruption?" No Pages. Cited 26 Nov. 2018. Online: https://www.transparency.org/news/feature/corruption_perceptions_ index_2016 table].